How to Become a Millionaire Health Care Worker

Vergara Dean

"A BOOK IS A DREAM THAT YOU
HOLD IN YOUR HAND."

NEIL GAIMAN

To LEILA

It all started in a dream, including writing this book.

Even my first and lifetime investment was once a wish

in a dream. Now, it's part of everything I am deeply grateful for.

You are indeed a priceless Gem.

To AUDREY and KATRINA

Thank you for allowing us to grow richer

and healthier in many ways.

To my MOM & DAD

Paciencia, a teacher, and Dr. Alvaro, a countryside

physician - your values and commitment are worth emulating.

Contents

INTRODUCTION

"We make a living by what we get,
but we make a life by what we give."

WINSTON CHURCHILL

CONGRATULATIONS! You have chosen a career in healthcare. The career may not be lucrative and flashy. But there is nowhere else in the world you can find a job humanely serving your fellow man, especially at his sickbed's most painful and helpless moment.

CAN YOU BECOME A MILLIONAIRE HEALTHCARE WORKER?

With a healthcare career, you are assured of a financially stable workplace, and you can earn more if you put in more working hours. You have chosen a field of work where you have a fair chance to thrive and become a millionaire. Moreover, you are best positioned to attract the world's goodwill with your compassionate and altruistic power.

Whether or not you become a millionaire, your career in healthcare will allow you to achieve some financial stability. Your pay rate and employer-sponsored benefits are comparable to those of workers in other fields. Anyway, it's not how much you earn that matters; it's how much money you can set aside and how you manage it that makes a huge difference.

WORDS ARE POWER

This is my first attempt to write a book. Some authors say a book title makes all the difference. I admit I spent more time choosing the first word than the title. I needed to open this book with a word that could spell a world of success. That word is CONGRATULATIONS.

Congratulations was the word I told myself when I first landed in the USA at JFK in New York. But it was not the word I blurted out from the airport after the yellow cab driver hastily dropped me at 150th Street in the Bronx and quickly drove off with my change. Congratulations was the word I said after I recovered from the shock. (I must confess, out of exasperation, I could not avoid adding a word or two you don't need to know.)

"Congratulations " means different things to people. I don't know what it means to you, but I want to congratulate you — not because you took this book. But because you are willing to change your financial situation. Time will tell how it transforms you. Believe that you can, and I do not doubt that you will.

The idea to write this book was born from seeing so many healthcare workers facing daily financial challenges simply because they lack a basic understanding of personal finance. I met many with post-traumatic stress disorder from ugly experiences dealing with debt collectors, foreclosure, bankruptcy, and legal hurdles due to financial mishandling.

For example, I witnessed a lot of colleagues juggling multiple credit cards. They do not participate in their company's retirement benefits, and those who set aside money for their retirement funds are not putting aside enough. I see an urgency to reach out to healthcare workers. That explains why I am writing this book.

I KNOW YOU: I CAN WRITE YOU UP

You may be asking how I learned so much about healthcare workers. Well, I've worked with them at various rungs and positions. I've listened and talked to them in the hallways, employee lounges, and conference rooms. I've joined them even at their houses during family occasions like birthdays. I've worn the uniform of an ER nurse, critical care nurse, and behavioral health nurse. I've also stepped into the shoes of a nurse manager and Hospital administrative supervisor. I came to know them well; I know their pains, laughter, smiles, and smells. (Also, I know how often they overslept past the end of their break time during night shifts.)

Before the pandemic, the Economic Policy Institute reported, on December 10, 2019, that "Most families, even those approaching retirement, have little or no retirement savings."[1] Healthcare workers are not removed from the realities affecting mainstream America. It is a matter of grave concern. We need to realize that our working years are numbered, and that number is getting smaller. You can ignore it, but retirement age will catch up with you. Plant your seed money now.

---

1   Morrissey, "The State of American Retirement Savings."

YOU DON'T HAVE TO BELIEVE ME. YOU HAVE THE CHOICE

I did not write this book to unearth a bag filled with a million dollars by mumbling archaic formulas. I do not hold a degree in finance and have had no formal studies in crypto-currency or stock trading. I am not even an investment expert or a financial planner. So you don't have to believe me. It's fine with me. I consider myself just an ordinary American healthcare worker who has discovered powerful financial tools and strategies (to grow a seed of money into a giant money tree) which until today remain hidden and unknown to countless people. I want to write them here to tell the world what I have found and applied — with remarkable outcomes.

WHY DID I WRITE THIS BOOK FOR YOU:

→   To introduce wealth-building strategies and common vehicles of investments such as bonds, mutual funds, stocks, and real estate investment trusts for their compounding growth potential. This book also dis-cusses tax-deferred accounts like Traditional IRA, Roth IRA, 401(k), 403(b), and 527b. You will also learn practical concepts related to money manage-ment and decision-making: opportunity cost, Rule 72, budgeting, compound interest, debt management, insurance, and saving for an emergency fund.

→   To introduce you to critical financial strategies and best practices to save money and leverage other peo-ple's technical knowledge and skills on investments, financial planning, and debt management to grow your money.

As a healthcare worker, learn to tap your altruistic power and compassion to attract the positive Karmic forces in your favor by making a positive connection to the world.

This book project has been culled from years of experience, insights, and knowledge as we build values. The book contains the nuggets of financial wisdom I have found throughout my journey as I followed in the footsteps of those who achieved financial success. My observations, research, and interviews with colleagues produced a wealth of information that is truly worth sharing. But remember: information on personal finance and investments in this book can also be found in other sources. I encourage you to expand your reading. Knowledge is a bedrock of financial success.

THIS BOOK IS SPECIALLY MADE FOR YOU

Throughout this book, I presented principles and concepts in a language YOU can understand, whatever your level of financial literacy. This book stands apart from others on the shelf by empowering you to adopt an entirely new mindset and apply those transformative financial tools and strategies to become a millionaire healthcare worker. After all, this book was written by a registered nurse who understands You by heart and your unique situation. Together, let us walk on the road to financial freedom. Congratulations!

ACKNOWLEDGMENT

"When I started counting my blessings,
my whole life turned around."

WILLIE NELSON

During our financial journeys, we met people who paved the way for us to overcome hurdles. I may need to remember their words spoken and written. But I can't. I can only write their ideas and draw faces.

When one writes a book, the writer lives forever. So a page of acknowledgment is an expression of the author being GRATEFUL forever:

To Helen Okwonko, RN, and Susie Larsen Sappington, my healthcare heroes at Unit - C in Riverside University Health System, Arlington Campus; to Kwame Appiah, NP, MBA, for sharing ideas (including the suggestion for the book title). Also, to Dean Audrey Vergara for book cover design.

Thanks to Frederick Sarpong, RN, NP, and Kevin Tombo, RN, for turning those otherwise dull shifts into enriching experiences.

Thanks to my Assistant Nurse Managers, namely: Joy Christian, RN, Chioma Okwonko, MSN, RN, and Toni de La Merced, RN, for constantly reminding me to have "coffee breaks" and "take a nap" during those nocturnal shifts. Likewise, to my hardworking Nurse Manager, James Cook, RN, MSN. Special thanks to Philip Penaflor, Ph.D. in Applied Cosmic Anthropology, for his valuable input in this book.

Wherever you are now — Dianne Discala and Eudelia Margostrino, Azineth Lo, Sandra Sarvida, Dr. Albert Novero, and Vilma. Likewise, to Mayet Salazar, Heide Mongcal, Joe and Pilar Diaz, Arsenia Ramirez, Jo and Rudy Lacson, Bing Ignacio, Linda and Bruce Sartain, Adel and George, and Tita Apol: thanks for having there for us, especially for looking after Audrey and Katrina when we were living in the Bronx.

Special thanks to George and Mildred Wilson, Rolly Tumaque and family, Rowena Ramos and family, Joseph Ibanez and family, Emmanuel Vergara and family, Belen Teves, Omer Ramos, Joel Oliver and family, Luis Co, Juvy Usero and family of Sugarland, Texas, for support and friendship.

Thanks to the following healthcare heroes (in any order): Thelma Beltran, Dr. James Tan, Monette Kliatchko, Aimee Encarnacion, Belen Teves, Andeli Areza, Olu Akintewe, Bancy Kahone, Dannie Mahinay, Grace Shiro, Rupert Torres, Dina Banawis, Shirley Bibera, Tiola Bays, Michelle Crisostomo, Doris Caudor, Amy Wang, Rose Effinger, Dr. Rolando Badayos, Emerson Guiyab, Mhor Tablit, Jonathan Ceralvo, Juliana Island, Soledad Kudsi, Carmen Moll, Sarah Matigi, Francis Nwanko, Victoria Osanyinpeju, Evangeline Reyes, Enriquita Sy, Neil Rosales, Joann Faisan, William Valdez, Dr. Pamfi Amores, Dr. Paul Lardizabal, and Dr. Pulido Wilbur. Likewise, thanks to Dr. Mary Ann Dee, MD, RN, and Dr. Victor Gallardo.

Thanks to my wonderful colleagues at Riverside University Health System. Likewise, to the wonderful nurses and staff at 5 East, Kaiser Hospital - Riverside, namely: Teresa Reyes, Gina Raymundo, April Santos, Lorelei Enalvez, Alona Gagnon, Dulce Castillo, Ruby Tejeda, Cristina Ojano, Emily Lopez, Sabrina Umali, Rachele Sarmiento, Benny Singh, and Anika Thao. Also, I am deeply grateful to their Wonderful Buddies - I'm the number 1 fan of Dennis Santos, Gilbert Reyes, Gene Raymundo, Eric Umali, John Gagnon, Nick Enalvez, Kenneth Ojano, and Chal Tejeda. It is poco de cielo!

Thanks to my former colleagues at Lincoln Hospital Medical Center ER in the Bronx, New York, and at Norwalk Community Hospital in California.

I thank my friends and colleagues who have shared their money issues and provided materials for this project.

Thank you, Rhoda Buntan, RN, and Eden Gayapa, RN, for recommending the cover color scheme; to Mary Lou Wilhelm and Fredi Morales of Riverside Public Library for manuscript enhancement. Let's dream and continue believing. Thank You.

Chapter 1

MONEY IS NOT
ROCKET SCIENCE

"If you are misguided and undecided, knowledge and
wisdom can be provided. Given that, we forget to
capitalize off of the fact that someone in the Universe has
already experienced the issue we are trying to overcome."

BENJAMIN MICHAEL, THE POWER OF YET (2019)

Life may be a complicated science from someone's micro-
scopic point of view. But money is not. Have you ever
wondered why some people—perhaps even among your
peers—have no issues with money, while others carry a
freight of money problems? For some, money is like a water
current flowing into their lap. For others, it is stagnant or dry.
Where lies the line? Do our earnings make any difference?

Our attitude or mindset, lack of basic knowledge of personal finance, and lifestyles affect our financial behavior,
not how much money comes in. Just like a first-year student
dreading his algebra, it's all in the attitude and lack of basic
foundation that the subject, like money, is an insurmountable
problem.

Before you found yourself in your messy financial situation, countless people were already there and had gone
through crushing financial trials. But many of those people

have successfully weathered and resolved their money issues and challenges, just as you are doing now. Chin up! You are greater than the sum of money in the world. But the more you focus on and preoccupy yourself with money, the more complicated it will seem. It can lead to the impression that money is rocket science, but it is not.

MONEY FLOWS LIKE A CURRENT: BELIEVE IT

Money was logically designed to flow or circulate like water in the stream. By its very nature, money moves, and flows, not stagnant. It moves, circulates, and follows its natural course to the places most receptive to its flow. There is no reason or purpose for the current to flow in any direction other than where it needs to be. To catch the flow of the current, you need to be in the right spot with a receptive frame of mind like a catcher positioning himself to seize the ball with his open mitt.

In China, the currency is called the yuan or renminbi. Renminbi means "the people's currency." In Japan, the currency is known as the yen. In the Philippines or Mexico, it is the peso. In India, the currency is the rupee. Here in the USA, it is known as the mighty dollar. Regardless of the name of the currency, the country, and its economic condition, currency means one thing: money. Money is currency.

The word currency has its roots in an old French word, courant, meaning "to run or move." It means money is a currency intended to move, circulate and flow. You must know the strategies to catch where it flows with the right tools.

In short, you need to know and apply the financial means and concepts with the right mindset to successfully draw the currency in your favor. Money thrives and grows when put to good use or invested and not kept stagnant. Because when you invest your money, spend it wisely, or put it to good use, you permit the cosmic energy of money to run in the right direction.

KNOWLEDGE OF TOOLS AND STRATEGIES MAKES A DIFFERENCE

I wear the same healthcare uniform that you do. But there's a difference between you and me. The difference is neither in what you clinically do nor what I don't do, nor how smartly you beat the tempo of the work clock.

I have discovered, learned, and applied the powerful financial tools and strategies to grow the seed money — that ordinary American workers have also learned and applied to nurture their seed money into a giant money tree. These workers have catapulted their way to becoming millionaires despite their ordinary or regular incomes. While I was fortunate to discover the tools and strategies of those who succeeded financially, it is unfortunate that these pieces of information remain hidden from countless people regardless of education, profession, color, and culture.

Again, I am not a financial expert and I do not hold a degree or even have a certificate in finance or investment. So you don't have to believe me. I did not write this book to persuade you. But if you do believe, good. Because you need to believe in yourself —you can become a millionaire. It would help if you believed that you could unlock your door to financial success. That is the first step to unraveling the "rocket science" behind money circulation.

IT'S NOT WHAT YOU EARN, IT'S WHY CAN'T YOU SAVE

It's not what you earn that matters to succeed in the game of personal finance. I am not interested in how much you make. I am not even concerned whether you are hard-working or just hardly working. I can't do anything with how much you deserve to receive. Instead, you should ask: why can't you save, and what can make you save?

I must tell you that you don't need a double college - major or even a single one— written beside your name to reach those seven figures in your account. Let's face it, countless people with a college degree are trapped in 8-hour jobs with nothing to show financially. Financial success is not the same as academic prowess. What matters is not what you earn, but why can't you set aside money from what you earned?

THE PERSONALITY OF MONEY

To understand money is to look at two faces of the same coin. One side must be understood in relation to your own needs, wants, priorities, beliefs, and values, including your emotions and state of mind. In contrast, the other side of the coin must be understood in the same context but in relation to other people — their needs, greed, wants, assumptions, priorities, beliefs, and values.

By looking at these two facets of money, you will understand the dynamics of money and the personality traits affecting the money cycle. Likewise, you will gain insight into how and who has the upper hand to pull the strings when money is involved.

As an employer, I have the upper hand on whether or not to give you a promotion and raise your rate. I command the price of something that you are interested in buying and which you think is worth more than your money (even if I think the same thing is worthless). I can control the price if there is only one repair shop in town. Labor unions and union negotiators have the upper hand in bargaining against hospitals in times of shortage of clinical skills like nurses.

By looking at the faces of the same coin, we can also understand the ups and downs of the market. The market will move because people on one side need money, are fearful of events affecting their money and investments, or simply have different outlooks and perceptions. On another side, people have different views and assumptions of the market and events or they are motivated by self-interest and greed. These can influence the market projection and the prices to rise and fall.

TO KNOW YOURSELF IS TO KNOW YOUR MONEY

You gain entry into the person's heart by how he values and uses his money, and you know how he values and uses his money by his character. Money is everything depending on the character of one who holds it and who needs it. Money is a powerful medium for obtaining another person's service or acquiring something that you perceive as equivalent to or greater than the value of your money. Money must generate mutual value and satisfaction for the parties involved in the transaction.

Money reflects your character, choices, priorities, values, beliefs, attitudes, and ability to discipline yourself. Your financial issues are consequences of what appear to be routine, insignificant, and non-essential spending which gathered momentum and dragged down your finances, just as your financial stability is the consequence of your mathematical calculation and smart use of money, including choices that generate greater value for you.

To understand money and your financial situation is to understand your personality concerning money. You cannot separate your personality from your money.

HEALTHCARE WORKERS AND THEIR CHALLENGES

Healthcare workers are hard workers. They are also good earners. But many are drowning in high-interest-rate credit cards, auto loans, large mortgages, and student loans. As a result, many work long hours and forfeit important family occasions to take extra shifts to meet due dates.

Healthcare workers are sleep deprived and overly extended without realizing it. Adding to their burden, many healthcare workers are financially obligated to provide for their families back home. This extended responsibility, coupled with their economic issues, is aggravated by the stress of their working environments. These bear an ugly emotional and psychological toll on their personal and family dynamics. No wonder divorce rates among healthcare workers, especially among nurses and doctors— are alarmingly high even as the general trend in the US is declining.

One good thing to note, health care workers have learned the art of hiding their issues behind their calibrated smiles as they deal with the problems of others. But to those of us who understand, their constant strain is palpable.

I don't believe in luck unless you define luck as another form of chance. I don't even believe in hard work as a way to get ahead in life. The word hard says it all: the work is hard. That is why it is called hard work. That also explains why we call that dude who works hard a "hard worker." Let's be honest: throughout your career, you've seen gutsy pinheads climbing the ladder and getting plum positions, or dwarfing their hard-working, educated, and skillful or talented colleagues who are stuck in their footsteps. That is reality 101.

IMPORTANCE OF STABLE DOMESTIC RELATIONSHIP

If you want to attract the flow of money, you must attract goodwill or a cooperative attitude toward you: be it in your career or relationship. As healthcare employees, we cannot talk about financial strategy and financial security separate from our job or career and relationship. You must have at least a stable job or career that offers better prospects with supportive people and management. In terms of relationships, a supportive and stable relationship is conducive to financial growth. It inspires success and the ability to take on calculated risks. An unstable domestic relationship can lead to break-up, divorce, or a fractured marriage. This instability can have a cascading effect on finances, causing erratic fluctuations in an employee's job performance during domestic disputes and stifling the flow of creative ideas. Even within companies that have supportive management, employees may develop an entrepreneurial spirit.

DON'T GET STUCK IN THE TRAFFIC OF LIFE OR CAREER

Many people driving cars would instead do nothing and wait for the traffic jam to clear. That's understandable. But if it's your life, career, or finances that become bogged down or get stuck, it's different, and the dynamics are not the same as your car being caught in a traffic jam. That's why your colleagues complain about finances, relationships, health, and poor career opportunities, yet they fail to realize they are getting stuck in the traffic or refuse to change lanes and forge their own path.

There is nothing wrong with these people. They are educated, talented, and hardworking. But after staying so long in the system or in the same condition, they are used to the traffic jam and their daily rigors. They've become pro-grammed to accept the whole gamut of their situation. That is how to reframe your mind by subjecting it to a litany of negative thoughts and eventually surrendering or accepting the thought that the situation cannot be resolved and nobody can do it. So now you accept your situation because that is how you reframed your mind. It's a vicious cycle.

I remember my friend, Jimena. She was passed over twice for promotion to Assistant Nurse Manager. Jimena has outstanding professional qualifications including clinical, and social skills. But her Senior Manager treated the workplace like a shoebox and does not appreciate the challenges of having variety inside the same box. Do not get me wrong. My friend is smart but dumb enough not to move out of the traffic jam to nurture her dream, bloom somewhere and earn more in the process.

If you hit a traffic jam, you don't just wait inside your car; you must at least try to resolve, and negotiate out of the trapped lane. Just as in life, you need to get out of the traffic or zone of no – growth to get ahead. After you reach the age of 18, how much time do you have to fix or do things to get out of your own traffic and reroute yourself if you fail? Life is short not to take risks and try new things that you will regret not having tried doing.

BE SMART: HARD WORK AND JOB LOYALTY ARE NOT ENOUGH

Familiarity and convenience are the enemies of change. To succeed, you need to be creative to recreate yourself. But creativity cannot come from someone resistant to change. A mind mired in the familiar and refusing change cannot be creative. Whether you're looking to grow your finances or advance your career, you will never find growth by safely doing the same thing repeatedly that has always brought you average results.

Again, as a healthcare worker, you cannot talk about money and financial growth without relating it to your source of income – your job, your workplace, or your professional practice.

Like your career trajectory, money does not thrive when hidden away in safety; it must move and flow like a water current. If you want to improve your situation, more than hard work and job dedication are needed. Be smart. Take calculated risks. Either change lanes or make your own. It takes guts to negotiate quickly through the slow traffic of your life. Don't surrender to the comfort of your safe but lousy gains.

MORE THAN A MILLION DOLLARS IN YOUR LIFETIME

A worker paid $25 an hour today can look forward to earning more than a million dollars during his career. That is not counting any pay increases, promotions, or movement with higher pay, and an additional income from working extra shifts, which is common among healthcare workers.

You belong to a stable healthcare ecosystem. That is a statement of fact. If you are paid biweekly, and you set aside around $167 per pay period, in one year, you will save $4,000. If you earn a yearly compounding rate of 8 percent, you can be a millionaire in roughly 30 to 35 years. Again, it does not include the money given by employers as a matching contribution (usually up to 5 percent of employee contribution) to their employees' retirement account, nor does it include any contribution increase you might make during your working years. With your employer matching contribution and gradually increasing your tax-deferred contribution, you can be a millionaire in about 30 years.

Your ability to attain your first million does not depend on the money you earn today; it depends on the aggregate of positive factors that can influence your money growth. For example, the power of compounding returns, time, financial behavior, or lifestyle affects your financial projection. Likewise, your chosen vehicles of investments, your emotion, and your frame of mind are all factors that influence your ability to grow your money.

If experience is the best instruction, let us learn from the experience of people who successfully weathered financial challenges that might be worse than those you face. Rich people are successful people. They know what they did to get there. Likewise, let us learn from those who dreamed and achieved the same thing you are trying to work on. They left the writing on the wall so that others could know that money management is not the rocket science we used to believe.

Chapter 2

STORIES HEARD
THROUGH STETHOSCOPE

"Rich people plan for three generations.
Poor people plan for Saturday night."

GLORIA STEINEM

The length of your journey to reach your first million dollars will differ from the journeys of others. For those born with a silver spoon in their mouths, a million dollars or more was just a cry from the cradle. For some, the journey is a sprint. For others, it's a pace. For the rest, it's years of running a seemingly rigged race with no end. I don't mind the pace. What matters is taking that initial step promptly with firm resolve.

This chapter will give you a glimpse into the financial lives of our healthcare workers. Some of their situations may mirror your own. The workers in these stories could be the guy doing the X-ray, the social worker mediating domestic issues, the respiratory therapist, or the pharmacy technician filling the Pyxis cartridges. They could be the phlebotomist drawing a specimen in the morning or even your colleague you love to tease as a pinhead.

I have changed the names of the workers in these stories but not the stories. First, let me share our story.

THE BRONX IS THE BIRTHPLACE

My baptism into American life as an immigrant started in the Bronx, New York. We lived on the second floor of a two-family brownstone house with a rentable basement. During winter, the owner turned on the heater for two hours twice daily, at six o'clock in the evening and six o'clock in the morning. I can still recall the faces of the basement occupants, then new arrivals from El Salvador. The first floor housed a family from Puerto Rico. The apartment building was a fusion of beautiful culture, except for the noise and loud music that sounded like speakers directed at me when it was time to bed.

The neighborhood was made intimidating by graffiti etched into the apartment doors, the walls, and even the cars parked on the street. I saw more cockroaches roving the hallways of my apartment than NYPD officers patrolling the street. It was a tough neighborhood in the Melrose section: then one of the poorest congressional districts in the USA. You would not dare to park even an old car overnight in this place. But the Bronx was the birthplace of a dream and an impetus for me to pursue the American dream.

Not far from our Bronx haven stand the skyscrapers of Manhattan, a short ride by trains 5, 2, or 4. As a young man and a newcomer to this country, those glass towers that almost reached the sky never ceased to amaze me. My mind would fly past those towers and wonder what kind of dreams the people living there had weaved to live so high up.

DAYDREAMING IN THE SOUTH BRONX

I love to watch the Manhattan skyscrapers. I told myself if they could build those glass towers that reach the sky, there

23

was no reason not to dream just as high. After all, dreams werre free and always will be. And this spark of imagination brought me to the doorsteps of Hostos Community College in the Bronx. I became a registered nurse (RN) with my wife's help throughout nursing school.

While we lived in the Bronx, my wife and I used to take our daughters to the affluent sections of New York City, Long Island, and Westchester. We visited these places to spend time at the Barnes and Nobles, dine at the local burger houses, window shop in their upscale shopping centers, or just stroll through the downtown streets without looking over our shoulders. These were the corners of the world where we could watch how affluent, successful, professional people shopped and dined.

My wife and I would let our kids loose in the bookstore's children's section. We would savor personal finance, other self-help books, and magazines for hours for free until late in the evening. We valued the importance of reading, which is how we were first introduced to personal finance. We learned about vehicles of investment and financial tools outside of just tax-deferred accounts.

In many ways, our marriage has attributes of a business partnership when it comes to finances. That's why my wife and I have always had "equal rights" concerning our money. We discuss our finances and share ideas on managing our resources like good business partners. It's a "give and take" and making sacrifices for the partnership. That also contributes to our happy marriage. A happy marriage attracts money.

In practice, we only kept enough money in the bank to avail of checking account convenience. Initially, I kept track of every purchase so we could monitor our expenses for two months. It was hard, but we needed to do it as part of the process. First, we took note of what we spent on certain items. Then we looked at the list to see what we could reduce or avoid altogether. We also regularly monitored the progress of our savings or investment. I believe a good recording of expenses and investments is a sound financial practice.

I increased our monthly savings or investment when I started earning as a nurse. I even sent my entire paycheck (or even more) to random investment companies. I found them after seeing their advertisements in a newspaper or financial magazine. Fortunately, they were genuine investment institutions: T. Rowe Price, Janus, Charles Schwab, and Baron Funds. The money I sent them was invested in stocks and mutual funds focused on domestic and international stocks and bonds. I took the risk. Money does not generate money without risk.

BE TRUTHFUL TO YOUR GOAL OR PURPOSE

I came to America on a visitor's visa; I wanted to visit American landmarks. But I saw more opportunities than places as a Tourist. I thought that the only route was going back to school when resources permitted. I wanted to succeed and unveil the enigma of the American dream. Today, I count myself as one of the countless economic immigrants with a career in health care.

Among close friends, I have no qualms in saying -- I decided to venture into America because I want to be rich. America is a rich country. There is no reason to be poor in one of the richest countries in the world. That fact alone was a stack to build on. I want to have a better life and have something to leave to my children. It's ugly to be poor, stagnant, or financially crippled while living in one of the richest countries in the universe (God Bless America).

HAVE YOUR AMERICAN DREAM AND BUILD ON IT

I am an economic immigrant — constantly in pursuit of the American dream. The American dream is personal to me: it means financial security and having something to leave to the next generation. The American dream also means giving back or contributing to America as a nurse for new dreamers to build on.

Always conscious of that dream, my wife and I observe prudence in handling our money and resources. Even with an income from two full-time nurses, we decided to remain on the same street in the Melrose section of the Bronx. Our apartment was a block from Lincoln Hospital and Medical Center, where we work, and half a block from the Catholic Church of the Immaculate Conception. Subway lines 4, 5, and 2 were a few hundred steps away. The apartment was a short walk to the commercial district of Third Avenue. My children attended a Catholic school run by nuns.

I rented out the extra room of our apartment to another nurse for $400, cutting our monthly rental from $900 to $500. It has lowered our housing expenses significantly compared to hundreds of thousands of US households that devote more than 40% of their monthly income to housing.

But one problem remained while we were in the Bronx apartment: we had a landlady from hell who yelled and refused to repair our fixtures. But looking at the positive side,

I learned two important lessons: to have a rental income and to be considerate to tenants no matter what.

In 2007, three years after I left the Bronx, that wish to be a Landlord became a reality when I bought a house in Las Vegas, Nevada. I became a landlord to a couple who rented our Las Vegas house. The tenants did not give me a headache. My secret? Every contract anniversary, I gave my tenants a small box of goodies or basket of groceries and a thank-you note for keeping the house.

My lease contract included the standard clause requiring the tenant to pay an additional 5% for any late rental payment. Once, the tenant sent in their rent with a 5% charge for the late fee. I mailed the extra payment back to the tenant with a note that said this:

"Thank you for honoring the lease contract by sending an extra $35. I'm returning the money to you, knowing an extra buck helps. As you know, I am also paying the mortgage for that house. Please be mindful of sending your rental check on time, or feel free to let me know of any problems. Thank you."

Unfortunately, buying that house in Vegas was like placing a bet in a slot machine. The house value fell terribly in the last great recession of 2008 – 2009. Holding on to the house to recover its value was like betting on the same slot machine and waiting for a lucky break. I needed to give it up.

As our investment grew in other accounts, so did our expenses. We were conscientious about our expenses. I would sometimes remind my wife, Leila, to cut our expenditures. She would snap, "Cut? Do you want me to cut my finger?" But it's not that we're tightwads; we're just smart spenders. We traveled with our kids to Europe, went on a cruise, and visited national parks and quaint American towns during summer. We traveled as a family outside the US every 2 years. Our kids attended Kumon after attending classes in private school. We regularly sent funds to our families back home and sent poor kids in the Philippines to school. We always set aside money for church and charities. We played hosts at our house countless times to friends and colleagues.

PURSUING THE DREAM IN CALIFORNIA

In 2003, we left Bronx, NY, to pursue our nursing career in California. But in 2002, a year before we moved, we decided to buy a house in California. We were bank-qualified for more than an $800,000 mortgage, which could have bought a stately home back then, but we decided to buy a $265,000 house in a gated community one hour east of Los Angeles. We had no regrets. Our monthly mortgage is much smaller than apartment rentals. The money we would have spent on a bigger mortgage for a bigger house went instead to our children's college funds through a 529 b plan and other tax-deferred investments.

When the house was completed in 2003, we finally moved to Southern California. My wife and I decided that while I worked full time, she would take a part-time position at a nearby Kaiser Hospital to devote extra time to our two daughters. Our children were our priority, rather than the earning potential of two full-time nurses. Fortunately, with due diligence, our investment returns were more than enough to replace what my wife could have made from a full-time job. In addition, through divine providence, our daughters, who stayed on the college campus during their studies, graduated without the burden of student loans.

Now, let us meet a few of our healthcare colleagues and learn from them:

1. Rachele Smalls, RN, 64 years old

Ms. Smalls complained of arthritic knees as she struggled to her feet after our meeting. She is 64 at the time of this writing. She looks forward to retirement but is anxious about her financial situation.

Ms. Smalls has worked in the behavioral unit of a government hospital for 11 years. She told me she is retiring in December, five months from now. She complained that she was always tired and in pain. In addition, she sustained a work-related injury two years ago. But she said, "I want to hang around to increase my pension. I'm afraid my retirement is not enough. But this COVID-19 virus is putting me in greater danger."

During our conversation, I detected no enthusiasm in her eyes about getting closer to retirement. She informed me that her Social Security benefits are estimated at $2,100 monthly. In addition, she will receive an additional $1,400 from the county hospital. When asked if she would also receive extra money from a tax-deferred account like 401K or 403b, she sighed and said, "I only contributed money there two years ago. Maybe I will receive a small amount of change." She added that she would receive a small amount from her old 401(k), which she had contributed for five years. "I have so many regrets," she said, " I should have contributed more to my old retirement account. But it's too late now. Five years are short."

Ms. Rachele Smalls admits that she failed to prepare for retirement. She is worried about her finances once she retires. Still, Ms. Smalls wants to retire in a few months anyway, despite her uncertainty. She pays $2,100 monthly for her mortgage on a three-bedroom house with $150,000 equity. She originally planned to sell the house, but the rent in the area is higher than her mortgage payments. She pays $430 monthly toward her car loan with a remaining balance of $19,000. She has two credit cards with a balance of $5,900 and the other card with $7,400. She sends her son $500 monthly to help him finish graduate school. Ms. Small is divorced. Her retirement money is tight, but she told me that selling the house and moving elsewhere would be too taxing. I could only wish her the best.

2. Sherrel Bondall, CNA, 36 years old
Ms. Bondall is a certified nursing assistant (CNA) who started working in her present job seven months ago. Her husband, Francis, is a pharmacy technician. I met Sherrel and her family at our colleague's birthday party. During our conversation, Sherrel told me that she used to work in a private skilled facility for 12 years before she got her present position in the local hospital. Curious, I asked her what she did with her old 401(k) or any tax-sheltered retirement accounts from her previous employer.

Sherrel regretted that she did not have one. But, she said, "Frankly, I don't know anything about the 401(k) or IRA you mentioned. Maybe the facility offered one; I don't know. I have heard about them but didn't have time for it."

The last time I saw Ms. Bondall, she told me she was glad she'd signed up for a 457(b), a tax-deferred account offered by her current employer.

3. Mr. Lucas Encinas, RN, 55 years old

My friend Lucas is an RN from Laguna, Philippines. His wife, Ruby, is 53 years old and an RN in a Subacute facility. I was invited to a small party for his 55th birthday at his house. Lucas has worked in a big hospital for 21 years. In addition, Lucas has an additional part-time job in another hospital, where he works two days a week and receives an additional $3,200 monthly. Lucas complained, "I haven't slept well for a long time. " I'm always so busy."

The couple's obligation on their daughters' college loan is about $70,000 and counting up (their daughter changed college courses a couple of times). They have a combined credit card balance of $15,000 at a 19% annual interest. The couple also has a $3,600 monthly mortgage on a five-bedroom house they bought for $625,000 in 2019. They have approximately $7,000 in the bank. Lucas admitted they did not promptly join their employers' tax-deferred retirement accounts.

Lucas is driving a 2022 Mercedes-Benz GLC with a balance of $60,000. That is on top of the couple's other $10,000 loan for the car their daughter is driving, which they pay $350 monthly. The couple relayed that most of the time, the two most common causes of their marital problems were money and not having family time. They added, "Money is still tight after all the bills and the children's school expenses are paid. We often have to borrow from our 401(k)." The couple has an estimated $300,000 in their combined retirement accounts. They have no other pension benefits from work aside from their separate 401k. Ruby said," We could hardly take vacations or enjoy free time. " Their only "nice family dinners" occurred at the local fast food in the area. They also send money to their relatives in the Philippines occasionally.

Lucas told me he was tired of working and felt his finances were not improving. After our friendly conversation over two bottles of Heineken, Lucas promised to look at their finances. He asked about financial planners in the area. He plans to retire at 62 when Social Security kicks in.

4. Ms. Peyrah Fardouke, RN, 29 years old

Peyrah is single. She started working as a staff nurse in the county hospital almost three years ago. That is her first nursing job. She said that her starting pay rate of $35 an hour job in a government-run hospital enabled her to finance a brand-new 2021 Nissan sedan.

Ms. Fardouke admitted she paid more than half her original $25,000 student loan. She aims to repay her student loan in the next two years. But when I asked Peyrah (her first name) if she has a tax-deferred retirement account, she answered negatively. "Somebody mentioned that sort of retirement account in the room during orientation, but it was not explained to us."

She also confided that she struggled to save even after three years as a nurse. Peyrah complained, "I have only eight thousand dollars in the bank—I cannot afford to save money. I'm paying off my student loan, and I have a car loan." She has a $3,800 credit card balance at 17% interest.

Unfortunately, six months after my last conversation with her, Peyrah had still failed to open a tax-deferred account offered by her employer. But she proudly talked about the progress she was making with her student loan. Still, she declared that her priority is saving money for her wedding.

5. Shannon Stevens, RN, 58 years old

Nurse Stevens started her nursing career in the State of Washington 16 years ago as an ICU staff nurse before moving to Los Angeles, California, in 2011. Shannon said she and her former husband worked their butts off until their relationship became messy. She added, "We came to the point where we were not seeing each other, and we were drifting apart." " We had no time for each other and we were trapped working."

Unfortunately, after 27 years in nursing, all she had were terrible memories of a failed marriage to a physician, including her federal tax arrears of $19,000 and California State tax arrears of $8,000, both of which were left in her lap after a non-contested divorce. Fortunately, she recently completed paying the state taxman by automatic deductions from her paycheck. In addition, Ms. Stevens has an estimated $45,000 in her bank from the proceeds of her old 401(k), which she closed and deposited in her savings account. Ms. Stevens also has about $75,000 in a 401(k) with her current employer.

She said she loves to window shop to "relieve stress," and she loves signature bags. She pays about $2,500 per month toward the mortgage on her house, which she made a significant down payment on in late 2018 through the help of a friend. Her house loan balance is $315,000 with small equity. She owes $11,000 over three credit cards with an average 20% annual interest rate. She still carries a car loan balance of $15,000. She works in two hospitals, one full-time and the other part-time. She complained that even if she received two paychecks every payday from her two jobs, her life would still be one paycheck away. She complained of getting tired; she plans to retire at 62, 4 years from now. Ms. Stevens said she went through bankruptcy and foreclosure ten years ago before buying the house. While discussing her retirement plans, she was teary-eyed and regretted mishandling her money and partly blaming herself for her divorce.

But Shannon promised to cut back on unessential spending and plan to work another year or two past 62. Like other medical workers, she has no other retirement benefits offered by her hospitals.

6. Ms. Bernice Goldstein, physical therapist, 49 years old

Bernice is a mother of three, and her husband, Donald, 50, is a Caseworker at the City social services. Their oldest child is 18 and attends a Catholic high school. Bernice has been working as a physical therapist for 17 years. She picks up extra shifts at the same rehab facility three to four times every month, giving her additional income averaging $2,800 after taxes.

She complained, "After paying our mortgage, my kids' high school tuition, and our credit card bills, nothing is left." The couple's combined balance in their bank joint savings and tax-deferred accounts is $85,000. She doesn't know how so much money slips out of her hands. She admitted that money issues were always the cause of their arguments. She admitted to having traumatic experiences with collectors and "legal people."

The family vacations outside the US every three years, most recently to Singapore, and sometimes spend weekends out of town. Donald drives a 2022 BMW going to work, and Bernice drives her 2019 Mercedes-Benz GLC. Bernice admitted that they could not afford to save for their retirement; they are always busy and they needed the extra money to meet their growing expenses. But they want to start saving at a later time.

In 2008, Bernice and Donald filed for bankruptcy when Donald lost his job. The couple skipped attending important school activities for their children when they were young because they needed to work extra shifts to cover their expenses. After exchanging notes and positive stories about financial successes, Donald was apologetic. He promised to contribute more to his tax-deferred account. Luckily, Donald has a defined pension plan at work where he will receive a pension for life at retirement.

HEALTHY HEARTBEATS OF SUCCESS: THEIR STORIES

Now, meet our other colleagues who are in different financial shapes.

1. Mr. Joshua Bridges, X-ray technician, 46 years old
Joshua is an X-Ray technician. His wife, Miriam, is a 48-year-old Licensed Vocational Nurse (known in most states as a licensed practical nurse). They met at Joshua's previous job, a subacute facility, way back in Texas. Joshua is a smart guy.

Joshua confided after they got married 19 years ago, the couple started putting money in their separate retirement accounts. Joshua told me that he and Miriam are good savers. When their first child was born, they started putting $400 every month into a 529 plan, a college savings fund. The couple increased it to $550 monthly after two years. They added another 529 accounts when their second child was born and put in $300 monthly. Joshua said, "We have a money plan and follow our budget. I don't want money to dictate us when I get older." The couple has two cars; one was purchased from a used car dealership. They carpool going to work.

While the rest of the staff in the hospital were talking about sports, fishing, and the various ways to get some promotion and earn an additional $2 an hour, Joshua and I always talked about other stuff like International events, stocks, investments, crowdfunding, and politics.

How much did the couple stash? They have more than $100,000 in their 529 college fund. They have a combined $595,000 parked in 401(k) accounts, plus an estimated $80,000 in a Schwab account invested in Microsoft, Starbucks, Bank of America, Disney, Amazon, and other stocks, I can't remember. The couple always paid off their small credit card debt every month. Their 3-bedroom house carries an estimated equity of $250,000. He said his wife earns about $35 an hour but seldom puts in extra work anymore. Josh still works extra shifts, but he channels all his additional income into their savings and mortgage so they can finish paying for the house when he turns 57. Joshua said, " I'm happy with our progress."

The couple always finds time to volunteer in their church and favorite local nonprofit organization. Joshua said they donate their time and give money to local schools and church fundraising activities. That is great!

2. Ryan Moll, RN, 53 years old, and Lea, RN, 50 years old
Both Ryan and his wife, Lea, are Registered Nurses. Ryan works in the local government–run hospital, and Lea is a part-time staff nurse in a private hospital. Ryan narrated, "We want financial security. We want to retire healthy and wealthy. I go to the gym regularly." " We have a budget. We plan before spending money on big items." Ryan admitted

they grossed "about $170,000 in 2022 from our jobs, investments, and interest." The couple put maximum contributions to their separate retirement accounts.

Ryan drives a 15-year-old truck. They are generous to charities and even sponsored a child's education through World Vision International. Ryan always treated his coworkers to boxes of doughnuts, Panera bagels, or pizza, especially when the shift was rough. Ryan said, "I don't care when nobody appreciates my gesture. My positive act matters, not what others did or didn't say." They sent two kids to college without any student loans.

Here is the kicker: The couple has a combined balance of over $990,000 in their employer-sponsored tax-deferred accounts, namely 403(b) and 401(k) accounts. Lea and Ryan have pension plans offered by their hospital employers aside from their 403b and 401K. They have over $140,000 in personal accounts invested in stock mutual funds. They have more than $11,000 in the bank. The couple pays a mortgage on a four-bedroom house with more than $300,000 equity. Ryan said that at one time, the balance of their 529 college savings plan surpassed $100,000. They prepared a college fund for their children to ensure they would not carry student loans. "Student loans are debt, no matter what." " We want to be millionaires at 62." Ryan was confidently smiling.

They take vacations outside the US every two years and regularly take long weekends and domestic vacations as a family. The whole family volunteers in the local church and at the Salvation Army feeding the homeless during Thanksgiving. "It is important to share our blessing with our coworkers, community, and church."

Their son will graduate from college in 1 year. In a few years, Lea and Ryan will be multimillionaire nurses—not even counting the equity in their house. Congrats!

WHAT CAN WE DRAW FROM THESE NARRATIVES?

Your income does not make an asset. The net worth disparity among our storytellers is not because of what they earned but how much they could set aside and how they managed it. Likewise, one thing that stands out - both Ryan and Joshua have a sense of purpose and social responsiveness.

SALIENT POINTS:

From the narrations, it is safe to draw the following conclusions:

→ Those who built assets more than the others have shown a sense of passion, consistency in saving money, and resolve to save. Joshua, the X-ray technician, said boldly: "We have a money plan. We follow our budget." He does not want money to dictate them. Nurse Ryan echoed it, " I want financial security. We want to retire healthy and wealthy." Both have shown clear financial direction and goals compared to others constantly on the grind.

→ You can see the big contrast in lifestyle and financial behavior among our storytellers. All storytellers work hard but only Ryan and Joshua stand out by showing a money plan and commitment to achieve their financial goals. They showed a common thread in social responsiveness as community volunteers and doing charitable works. They are even generous to their colleagues in the workplace.

REMEMBER:

Your small expenses, when added together, will become a mountain that's difficult to overcome on a credit card.

→ Make a budget for your regular household items such as electricity, water, cable, and food. Limit your expenses within your budget. Having a budget and financial goals prevents impulsive buying. Don't think of the budget or don't make goals only concerning big-ticketed items, future projects, or just because you plan to take a vacation.

→ When you make a budget, allow for miscellaneous expenses, then follow it. Make a budget based on your net income. Your net income is the money left after taxes and other deductions made by your employer.

→ Create an emergency fund for unforeseen expenses like a broken AC, a car breakdown, or an emergency room visit. An emergency fund of at least $2,000 can help avoid headaches and financial disruption. For a major emergency like a job loss, long-term sickness, or disability, financial planners recommend an emergency fund of at least three months to six months multiplied by your total household monthly expenses. Keep this fund in a separate account in your community bank or credit union. See Chapter 10.

→ Maximize your contribution to your employer-sponsored tax-deferred account. Anyway, you can always reduce or change your monthly contribution anytime. Your contribution to a 401(k), 403(b), or 457(b) will lower your taxes. Average Americans focus on how much of a refund they can get on their taxes at year-end, while the wealthy focus on how they can minimize taxes. See Chapter 17.

→ For your children's college expenses, contribute to a 529 account. In some states, your contribution to a 529 account is tax deductible. See Chapter 21.

→ Educate yourself on personal finance and various vehicles of investment like mutual funds, bonds, stocks, and other tax-deferred accounts. Learn about the dynamics of money management, including opportunity cost, time, and compounding returns, which significantly affect your life and finances. Husband and wife must be able to talk freely and equally about family expenses and investments. See Chapters 4, 5, 6, 7, 8, 9, 10, 11, 12, 13, 14, 15, and 16.

→ Ride in the success of others. Leverage the time, knowledge, expertise, and experience of professional fund managers. Leverage means using a device or some strategic means to easily pull or carry a big load with less effort or expense. When you leverage, you use small capital or monthly contributions to invest in mutual funds and stocks of the best companies in the world through these fund managers. To use this strategy, consult and work with certified financial planners (CFPs). These advisers are like coaches in the field of personal finance. See chapters 16, 17, and 18.

→ When things are hard to come by, reframe your Mind to change the game in your favor. Take calculated risks, and always know what those risks are compared to the benefits that will come out. Empower yourself by aligning your mindset to your plans and purpose. Experience the power of positive thinking. See chapters 3 and 7.

→ Attract the positive karmic forces in your favor — give, volunteer, and donate. Experience the rewards ordained by universal law by practicing generosity and social responsiveness. See Chapter 22.

→ Work with an employer that gives you a lifetime pension known as a defined benefit retirement plan. Many private employers are eliminating this excellent employee benefit, citing its maintenance cost. However, state, government agencies, and City run hospitals still offer Defined Pension Plans. If you are a poor saver, it behooves you to find an employer that will pay you a monthly pension during your lifetime. After your death, the benefits will extend to your survivor and beneficiaries.

Chapter 3

IF NOTHING WORKS, REFRAME YOUR MIND

"What you think, you become. What you feel, you attract. What you imagine, you create."

BUDDHA

Let me tell you. You are what your choices are. Your choices are your decisions. Successful people make better decisions and choices. Rich people made smarter financial decisions and choices. We cannot change our past choices and decisions. But today, we can make better choices and decisions with better outcomes.

Your thoughts and how you perceive events, your self, and what surrounds you shape your choices and decisions. Change your frame of mind, and you change your perception and way of thinking. A positive attitude makes positive thoughts.

If you find yourself working in the Behavioral Unit, with all the attendant risks to you, for a rate of $60 an hour as a Registered Nurse, that is your choice. You could have chosen to work in the Critical Unit that pays you a much higher rate. Also, if you decide to buy a new car with extra features, that is your choice. You could have purchased a used car and saved the difference.

This chapter emphasizes the importance of having a positive attitude or mindset. An attitude is an outlook. It is a mindset or how you framed your mind. A positive attitude is instrumental to financial success and in resolving many issues affecting your career, business, health, and relationship.

MINDSET

Your mindset is your unique personal perspective or attitude toward yourself and the universe born out of your experiences, values, biases, beliefs, assumptions, and knowledge. Similarly, by saying frame of mind, it is how you put them together or define your values, biases, beliefs, assumptions, knowledge, and experiences concerning yourself and the world. Like a picture frame, our frame of mind can either enhance the image of ourselves and our universe or distract us when looking at those images. Our frame of mind is our mindset, just as our mindset is our frame of mind. Whatever you call them, I treat them the same. How we frame our mind has bearings on our choices and decision-making process. The rich and the poor, the winner and the loser, have a mindset that affects their choices and perspectives. But it is how they frame their minds that separates the rich from the poor, and the winner from the loser.

MONEY MUST FIRST EXIST IN THE MIND

Perhaps you are asking, why not go straight to the numbers and dollar signs? What do these philosophical talks on mindset, choices, and decisions have to do with money and becoming a millionaire? The answer, my friend, is this: even a million dollars or two in your hand will not make you a millionaire.

A man is not poor just because he has no money or means to buy necessities and other requirements. A man is poor because of his mindset. Millionaires have a millionaires' frame of mind just as successful people have succeeded first in their mind before they become in the process.

Yes, the dollars and figures you desire must be written first in your mind before they can become real. Firmly believed and affirmed that you are what you will be. You must be successful first in your mind before you can attain success outside of yourself. Success must first exist in mind. You must have a millionaire mindset before you can become one. If you think you are unprepared, inadequate, and have an aversion to risk and responsibility, in that case, you cannot succeed in the real world.

Determination is a form of mental fitness. The ability to think and make good choices, including your attitude and self - discipline are mental craftsmanship. They are not your kind of muscular attributes. Instead, they relate to your mental strength, the pillars of success.

As I mentioned, becoming a millionaire is no small feat. Rich people are financially successful people. To join their ranks, you must have what it takes to succeed.

Condition your mind and envision yourself as the reality or experience you want. That is the power of reframing your mind or resetting your mind. It is no different from a young girl who wants to become a nurse or a doctor. She is what she wants to be not only in front of the mirror but also in her vision long before she even enters the school.

You have heard of people who desired to improve their financial situations and engaged in reading self-help books.

You've heard of others who attended classes on finance and money management. Many of these self-help books and financial gurus out there are truly outstanding. They prescribed and taught success strategies and financial coaching advice, including the latte formula, meaning you must scrimp on Starbucks coffee to save dollars. They are good at crunching numbers. Many authors boldly promise to make you a millionaire. I've lost count of how many authors told us we could achieve financial success. But what happens to the readers who follow these promises and assurances? Why are all these people back in the same rut? Why do they fail to resolve the same money issues despite their good intentions and knowledge gained from those books and coaching classes? That is similar to people who enrolled in Waistless 32, the hot new gym in town. (If you haven't heard of it, don't worry. There is no such gym.) These hopeful members were dedicated at the start, sweating it out, eating fewer carbs, and doing everything they should. But why do they quit before they're able to lose the weight that makes them feel unfit?

Why do others end up gaining more weight instead of losing it? Because something big is missing. They cannot find it in the books they read or the classes they attended. No, there is nothing wrong with the gym's weighing scale. However, something is missing within them; a chasm exists between their mindset and goals. Remember, knowledge and good intentions are not enough. Your feelings, beliefs, and actions must also harmonize with your plan.

Do you have what it takes to turn your vision and goals into reality? Do you have the risk tolerance, attitude, patience, temperament, values, and discipline to carry out your vision or goals? Don't let a disconnect between your mindset and goals hold you back. Instead, make sure you have the right frame of mind for success.

SELF-AWARENESS AND SUCCESS

You cannot continue working and taking extra shifts, thinking you are getting ahead financially by doing so. In the previous chapter, we have seen our colleagues doing just that, but eventually getting burned out, uninspired with soured relationships, and dragging their feet to work without bank accounts considerably bigger than those who have time to redraw and do other things. People succeed, fail, or remain in the humdrum, depending on how they chart their courses and revisit their progress toward their direction. As a healthcare worker, you cannot just keep grinding without directions and remain clueless about when to rest and when to proceed. Pause. Take a seat and reflect on yourself. Be wise and assess your relationship with the world around you. See what you need in order to move forward with a positive outcome.

As a healthcare worker, find a practical connection as to why your employer offers the annual clinical skills day: it is held yearly to revisit and review your clinical skills and relearn policies. Because as a clinician, you cannot just continue working without retooling yourself and making sure you know what you need to safely do the job. That is the same thing in all life pursuits.

Unfortunately, we do not usually know our fears, biases, values, attitudes, emotions, and temperaments. Self-awareness is understanding or learning about yourself, your beliefs, limits, and your outlook and applying it to reframe your mind or realign your thoughts to succeed. Like a device enabling the driver to navigate in the right direction, you must reset your mind to direct you to your destination. Calibrate your mindset just as you need to do with your car device. So first, we must look inward to examine whether or not we have the proper mental framework to succeed.

We can talk about investments, stocks, and dollars, including the financial strategies you'll learn throughout this book. They are meaningless if your mindset is incompatible with success itself. Nothing positive will happen if you're stuck with the same old misconceptions, beliefs, assumptions, and deep-seated biases. Remember, you are aiming for financial success— no small feat! Therefore, you must know and retrofit your mindset to remove the barrier to success.

THE POWER OF PLANNING, HAVING GOALS AND DREAMS

One problem with many people today is that they become floaters once they reach a certain point in their lives — like relationships, finances, or careers. People are floaters when they get used to their routines. They become numb and disengage from their conditions. They stop returning to the drawing board to map out the course or find an alternative way. It is worse to stop dreaming, making goals, and stop aspiring for something else. It is worst to stop believing in the power of dreams and goals. Your dreams and goals are wings to make you fly again.

Amidst poverty in the Melrose section of the Bronx, I weaved a dream to create a better life for myself and my family. I didn't even care if I had no "papers" back then. So, likewise, aspiring for a good life does not require " a paper." All I knew was that I was free to aspire and dream.

DREAM, PLAN, AND HAVE PURPOSE: KEEP THEM ALIVE

Do not stop weaving dreams. Keep your dreams alive. Keep making goals and plans. Obey them. Maybe it's a long-term goal like buying a house, pursuing a graduate degree, or raising money for your child's college. Regardless of how significant or small your aspiration, plan, or goal may seem, it serves as the driving force that gives you motivation, even on difficult days. They are like a "fire in your belly" that energizes you to get to the shower and drive to work even on a freezing winter morning. Our goals and aspirations empower us and provide a sense of purpose. They set the direction for our future. Likewise, your financial plan or goal serves as a compass of your financial behavior or choices involving money.

CONNECT YOUR MINDSET TO YOUR FUTURE

Our goals, aspirations, plans, and visions are mental figments or images of the future we desire or plan for. These future mental figments exist in the present as we create or formulate them. But they exist only in the mind as visions or images of what we want to become or have.

Example: Today, I plan to travel to Paris and aim to save $1,000,000 at retirement. The $1,000,000 and my Paris trip do not exist. Because they belong to the future as a goal or plan, except that they live or exist only in my mind as I formulate or make travel plans or saving goals.

Our goals, visions, and aspirations are expressions of the future reality we want to create, or we want to become. Our actions and words are powerful tools to connect the present to the future we want to have or achieve. Nature ordained us to succeed.

By aligning our minds to focus on the future reality we desire to achieve, our minds and the seemingly distant future become united. Unity is created within us as a unity of form and substance. We can powerfully and positively affirm to ourselves what we truly believe in and the direction we want to pursue. Self-affirmation evokes emotion, and positive emotion is positive energy. When we have positive feelings towards something we like or believe in, we are attracted to the thing or drawn to it and we act to make it real. Our actions and words are exact, determined, and calculated to succeed.

WE SHARE IN THE CRUMBS OF THE UNIVERSE

You stand out above the crowd in reference to no one. Even the person against whom you compare yourself also stands no bigger when compared to others. We all have the same footing in the Universe. It is our choices and outlook that differ us from one another.

Andrew's $100,000 is a bag of peanuts to Brando, worth $3 million. But Brando's $3 million is just a morsel to Charlie's $120 million. Likewise, Charlie's $120 million is just a speck in Mr. Bill Benzo's $50 billion. So take note: even the wealthiest man's billions of dollars in assets are crumbs of the wealth of the universe.

Wealth is seemingly an enigma. One can have so much that so many others do not have. Wealthy people can be found everywhere, just as people wallowing in poverty. Wealth is universal, and so is poverty.

Everyone shares in the universality of wealth. However, the individual share in the universal pie depends on the measure one puts on himself and how many miles he is willing to walk for it. As an employee, building your net worth must not solely depend on the price tag of your labor. Because employees or workers are underpaid, the tip of the scale always favors the employers. That is why looking out for and grabbing opportunities elsewhere that offer higher pay and better benefits is essential. Set aside money from what you earn and let it grow.

You have a choice. Don't get stuck in a stagnant place that offers no growth opportunities. Position yourself on the spot where you can catch or gather more crumbs of the wealth of the universe by saving money, having the proper place of work, career, and investments, and making intelligent financial decisions.

A DOUBTFUL MIND IS A CLOUDED MIND

It's essential to proceed with confidence. Your outlook on the universe will be hazy if you have a doubtful mind. Your perspective on the world reflects your blighted view of yourself. Doubt and indecision hide opportunity. An insecure or pessimistic mind creates an illusion of fear, bias, and risk aversion.

Unfortunately, doubts push you to hesitancy and prevent you from engaging. As French novelist Honoré de Balzac noted, "When you doubt, you give power to your doubt." That is why we are afraid to engage and get wet. So turn on the light. Learn and know what stuff makes people succeed. Educate yourself on money matters. Let go of the pain of financial ignorance that clouds your vision and serves as a barrier to resolving your money issues. As to your career, continue learning new skills and knowledge. Knowledge is a light to your path.

YOUR MIND CREATES YOU

You are what your mind has created you. Because that is what you thought or conceived of yourself and your world. Your mind creates you. It is the foundation of your success or failure. That is true for your career or profession, relationship, or health. You cannot expect a job promotion if your mind is tied to the mindset of a menial worker. You cannot climb the company ladder if your fear of heights prevents you from leading others from the highest rung. Don't expect to be given a position with greater responsibility if you have an attitude refusing even small responsibilities. Your poverty mindset will prevent you from becoming a millionaire because it disconnects your mind from achieving financial success.

Your mind is powerful enough to create the person you want to become, just as your mind can transform you into someone you did never want to be in the first place. No one wants to be poor. Even if given a million, a poor man will remain poor unless he changes how he frames his mind. If you want to be happy and positive, embrace positive feelings and ideas about yourself, and choose a positive outlook on the universe. You will find a balance and see through the window of opportunities. Enrich your mind to enrich yourself.

Your mind is a powerful key to your success. How you see yourself and how you assess the world are your choices. Carl Jung said it well: "I am not what happened to me. I am what I chose to become." We can reframe our minds and shape ourselves into who we want to be.

The notion that the ticket to wealth is winning the lottery or earning big money is just wishful thinking. It is not always true that people with high salaries or those who make millions are wealthy (or stay that way). We've all heard of high earners—people who were paid millions in salaries and bonuses—who ended up financially broke and heartbroken. Many have ended up in bankruptcy court. Likewise, more than 96% of multimillion-dollar lottery winners had ended up in a financially worse situation than before they bought the ticket to that magic ball. Many others have suffered personal setbacks or family discord they would never have dreamed of.

Do you know why such a high percentage of lottery winners, even some celebrities who have earned millions, ended up poor and broke? Is it because they bought luxury cars or yachts and stately homes? Is it because they have gone on exotic and expensive vacations? Is it because they threw too many parties for families and friends or because they invested in some business that went south? So what if they spent big on houses and a yacht? So what if they threw parties here and there or occasionally invested their money in a losing business or investment? They could afford to buy, and they could afford to lose — just as the other millionaires.

No, those were not the reasons why so many rich people and lottery winners ended up broke. On the contrary, they acquired multimillion-dollar assets when they bought those expensive yachts, cars, or stately homes and threw those large parties. They built social connections that the poor and middle class do not have. What they did after receiving those winnings, large incomes, and where they ended up are symptoms of who they became. They did not have the mental fitness and skill to handle such a sudden huge amount. How you manage your money, big or small, requires skill and mental fitness.

Many people need help to achieve financial success because there is a disconnect between their mindset and the reality of wealth. Cultivating a perspective more remarkable than the value of your desired success is essential. As Jim Rohn said, "What is important is the person you have become in the process of becoming a millionaire." In his book The Richest Man in Babylon, George Clason also emphasized the importance of learning and personal growth in accumulating wealth. He wrote, "This is the process by which wealth is accumulated; first in small sums, then in larger ones as a man learns and becomes more capable." In other words, you must mold yourself into the reality you want to create.

USE THE POWER OF AFFIRMATION

I remember my colleague, Deressa, an RN. She loves to call us 'honey.' She is sweet as honey, except when her patients or coworkers are giving her a hard time. Deressa told me that before she and her husband bought their marital house, her husband was helping to support the family. However, for whatever reason, he stopped working and became dependent on her for support. He has refused to find work. Deressa wants to take her husband to the Philippines and is planning to involve him in the Tulfo show, a popular TV program in Manila similar to The Jerry Springer Show. The reasons for her decision remain known only to her.

Deressa looks fragile, but she is an iron-willed woman. She said she paid the $200,000 mortgage on their three-bed-room house in less than eight years. She was categorical: "I was determined to pay my mortgage within ten years, and I believed I could. "Would you believe I paid my mortgage in less than eight?" I could feel her conviction in her voice. Deressa's demeanor showed her strong affirmation of what she believed she could do.

TAKE OWNERSHIP OF YOUR FUTURE

In our earlier days in the Bronx, New York, my wife was the only one working. Making both ends meet was difficult, especially after a second child. I could not work, and I was in nursing school. If I did work, the money I would have earned might be barely enough to pay the babysitter for my daughters.

Our financial situation did not deter us from setting goals or plans, such as returning to nursing school and putting money aside for investment. I set up a target amount or projected amount to be met, for example, every two weeks, three months, or a year. Although I wasn't working yet, every January – the first month of the year – I would write the pro-jected figure or target amount of money we wanted to meet at the end of the year. For example, for one year, I wrote $55,000 as projected savings. I also wrote to save $2,000 as the target amount every two weeks and $20,000 as pro-jected savings within four or five months. Again, my wife was the only one employed at the time I wrote those projected savings, and we even had difficulty meeting both ends. But at that time, if we could set aside $200 in a week, it was a big amount already for us— how much more saving $2,000 in a week or $20,000 in three or four months. But we did it!

As our savings gradually increased, I increased our projected figure to "set aside $3,000 weekly." Then, when I became an RN and worked in the ER at a nearby Lincoln Hospital, I increased our projected or target saving to $10,000 weekly or 60,000 in four months. As time passed, I began to write figures for $1,000,000 and more. It seemed fast, more fun, and it was exciting. We were millionaires even way back in the early days in the Bronx.

My secret? I always added an extra zero to the target amount I wrote. For example, by adding that extra zero to $200, it became $2,000. When I hit the amount as projected, I gladly imagined I set aside $2000 in a week. I was not only daydreaming (and looking crazy) but also changing my frame of mind to change our situation. A well-known author, Steve Maraboli, said," If you change your mindset, everything on the outside will change along with it." By adding that extra zero to the figure, we also claim ownership of our future or the goal we want to have. I was way ahead of our $200 weekly goal. Also, by adding an extra zero to the $300, which we could hardly afford to set aside (and quite a lot for us back then), the $300 became $3,000. Likewise, adding an extra zero to $100,000 became $1,000,000. The mind was framed to go for something bigger. It tricked the mind and excited the senses. The process of achieving the goal or plan was fun and invoked positive emotion and thrill. Which one would you instead want to have — $100,000 or $1,000,000?

Believe me, if you can see your goals with your eyes or have a clear mental image of what you want to achieve, self-affirmation empowers the mind to come up with amazing outcomes beyond your physical limitations. So reframe your mindset to change the game in your favor.

But there was a problem with adding that mystical zero. When my wife saw the figures I had been logging in, she demanded a place in upscale Westchester County and a Maserati. I whispered to her that these numbers were for the eyes only, and we laughed together. Our laughter brought even more positivity to what we wanted to accomplish. Yes, it may sound crazy. Call it whatever you want. Galileo, Robert Kayosaki, Steve Jobs, and Elon Musk - were once called crazy. What about you? What are you crazy for?

YOU ATTRACT WHAT YOU ARE ATTRACTED TO

Experience tells us that we have a positive feeling when we like something. In the same breath, we are easily attached or attracted to the object we want. So we tend to nurture the thing that attracts us and take positive actions to draw it to us.

Someone who sees his dream car displayed in the showroom will love to touch it, sit on it, or perhaps revisit the display room even if he cannot afford to buy the car because he likes it more than any other car. That is the power of positive emotion developed concerning what you want. I call it the power of attraction. Your words and actions are focused on what you are attracted to. Your words and actions connect your present goals and desires to the thing you want to have, or you want to be.

You attract something that you are attracted to. Because the power of attraction comes with the power of reciprocation by natural design, this is to breathe a balance in the Universe. By reciprocation, I mean it is an expectation that your efforts to draw attraction will either be positively returned or the thing itself will be drawn to you in some mutual fashion. Attraction involves positive emotion. Emotion is energy. Positive emotion invokes a positive reaction. Attraction invokes a reciprocal response.

Back in the Bronx, we used to tug our kids to the upscale New York City, Westchester, or Long Island sections. Those places were pricey. Even a burger from a fast-food chain was two times the price of the same burger sold in the Bronx. But I knew it was worth the money and time to experience some luxury by going right up to those places—to feel the life and the kind of energy of the most affluent and flourishing people we wanted to strive toward.

There is nothing wrong with spending to nourish the dream and the spirituality within us. However, being inspired or nurtured is a costly undertaking. The positive feelings and the taste of the finer things we experienced by being around those people in those places did not come for free. Those people were already living in their realm of reality while we were dreaming of the reality they already have. In short, we were dreaming the dream, but they were already living the dream.

One time my wife and I (together with our kids) tried to dine in a restaurant in the upscale area of Westchester in New York. For me, it was worth the money to smell the place, to observe how one man smirked and how another guy brightened his eyes at the sight of what looked like a (now) Wagyu, while we were feasting on what we could afford — a macaroni and cheese, a macaroni soup, and a salad. I remember the waiter asked, " Do you want to add

Chili Macaroni? " Frankly, I did not even understand what the question meant, what I did understand everything on the plate was pricey. We wanted to experience the atmosphere and smell of the place, even though we could hardly afford most of the dishes. You don't need to skimp on something delightful or worthwhile just to save money. The whole experience was worth the price. The experience of the good feelings associated with the occasion was the kind of reality we were trying to attract.

Spending time in those upscale places, window shopping in their glitzy malls, or simply dining in at the local fast-food chains was like a foretaste of the good life we could only dream of. For someone striving to achieve the American dream, it was a way to ignite the imagination. Let me tell you, aspiring for a better life feels futile if you can't appreciate the abundance you see in others. Similarly, working diligently and reaping financial rewards becomes meaningless if you're averse to the outcomes of your hard work.

MENTAL POVERTY: IT'S WHAT MAKES ONE POOR

It's not necessarily negative if you find yourself 'broke' or 'poor,' especially when you're trying to recover from setbacks like job loss, health issues, or other circumstances beyond your control. The real concern arises when you're in a state of poverty due to mental limitations. The term 'poor' can hold different meanings for different individuals. It's often used to describe situations where individuals lack the financial means or resources to fulfill their needs and basic requirements.

Poor or poverty is a complex word and does not just involve the lack of money or resources but involves the state of mind of the poor person himself. Not having cash or enough resources to meet one's needs may be temporary. But suppose poverty comes from choices, beliefs, or the outlook of one's self and the world? In that case, a deeper issue of a poor mindset cannot be resolved even if you give money to people experiencing poverty.

Money does not remove a person from poverty. Money flows. Poor mindset or mental poverty frames poor people to poverty. It is more restricting than being confined in prison. Austrian Philosopher Ludwig Wittgenstein wrote (Culture &Value, von Wright & Winch, 1977.), " A man will be imprisoned in a room with an unlocked door that opens only inward, as long as it does not occur to him to pull rather than push." In the same way, a poor man is locked into poverty as long as he thinks the lack of money causes his situation rather than his poor mindset.

The effects of a negative mindset are corrosive. It seeks company from indecisive, unmotivated individuals or those with the same attitude. Mental poverty itself is a trap.

A poor mindset or mental poverty is developed through time and experiences. Mental poverty begets a limited and dim outlook of the world. It is hard to recognize people with a poor mindset. You may not even recognize your own. It can be masked by alibis, blaming others, excuses, citations of facts, and arguments. But their actions will always betray them, rather than their words. Their choices will show their substance.

People with mental poverty think the universe has short-changed them or deprived them of the necessary life attributes to succeed. Their minds are framed in terms of immediate gratification, inadequacy, scarcity, hardship, doubt or insecurity, and mediocrity. So they tend to blame others and offer good excuses. They tend to hold onto things even when they hold no value. Additionally, they tend to believe it is too difficult to advance in their careers or professions. They project their mental poverty onto others. They think people are difficult, less generous, or unwilling to help. In practice, they also tend to be critical and less charitable of others, except those in their family or selected group. They cannot afford to extend the table to others, not their own.

In practice, you hold on to the safety of your bank deposits rather than taking a reasonable risk and allowing your hard-earned money to work. Because your money was hard-earned, do you think it needs rest?

LANGUAGE OF MENTAL POVERTY

People with a poor mindset have a language of their own. Wealthy and successful individuals, even those who are highly driven or motivated, speak differently compared to those who embrace pessimism, defeatism, or feelings of inadequacy. Believe it or not, our words connect us to the universe. Language is the bridge that allows people to communicate and connect seamlessly. Yes, actions do speak louder than words. But communication is not always conveyed in gestures alone. Remaining silent and inactive can disconnect you from others. That is the value of our words — they serve as the conduit that effortlessly links us to the universe.

People often say things like, "I'm broke. I have no money," "I'm poor," "I can't do it," " I'm just this or that." They might also say " I'm just a small guy here" or ask, " What does it have to do with my job?" These words indicate a condition of weakness, defeat, disengagement, indifference, self-humiliation, lack of enthusiasm, stagnation, scarcity, or absence. While they can reflect a temporary lack, they still carry negative connotations. It is worse when our words come from a mindset of powerlessness and mental poverty. Our negative words will continue to feed our negative minds. Our negative minds will continue to drum up those negative words. It is a vicious cycle.

Ninety-nine percent of what we can potentially achieve, fail to do, or refuse to do, especially in the workplace, has nothing to do with our position. You have the ability to take initiative, inquire, or approach someone in a higher rank who has the authority to undertake what you might not be authorized to do.

Words and actions can displace us from seizing and grasping the falling crumbs of the wealth of the universe. So, refrain from using the language of mental poverty — saying things like "I have no money" or "I'm broke" especially when you have (or will eventually have) money but it's not allo-cated for something in the current moment. The language of mental poverty has no cultural, religious, racial, or national boundaries. Those with a mindset of success and wealth will not understand you and may distance themselves from you. Conversely, individuals who share the same language of mental poverty will be drawn to your company.

It isn't pleasant to hear these statements from a working adult. It's uglier when your children listen to you using this rubbish financial language of poverty. Your children deserve to hear money spoken in positive and realistic language, not words reflecting poverty.

If you are genuinely "broke," "don't have money," or "can't afford" something you want, be truthful and remain positive. Express it more accurately:

→ "I like it, but it's not a priority."

→ "I'll need to budget for that"

→ "I don't want to use my credit card for this"

→ "We plan to pay for it in cash."

→ "I have money, but not for that."

→ "I have another priority right now; this can wait."

→ "I'll save up for it and buy it when the time is right."

→ "I need to negotiate for a discount."

These statements and others using the words cash, budget, value, saving, priority, and time are more realistically aligned with the language of finance and suited to sound money management. Moreover, people who hear you will admire your honesty for saying what they could hardly speak.

YOU ARE POOR IN RELATION TO THE OBJECT YOU DESIRE

You have been in your job for 5 or 15 years (probably more). But you keep saying you are broke or poor— do you have no money? No, you are not broke. When you say, "I'm broke," "I have no money," or "I'm poor," you are saying it about the object you desire to buy. You are not poor just because of what you cannot afford. Think about it. Why are you saying you're "broke" or "poor" if you are fully employed and have a steady source of income? That's an ugly mentality to put in your head. Now, reset your mind. You will see the difference within you.

A rich man with a net asset of $10 million is a multimillionaire. Still, he can be as poor and feel incapable as you or anyone else when he says, "I cannot afford to buy that $17 million house on an island." Someone with $18 million also "cannot afford" or is "too broke to buy" a $23 million house on another island that the other rich man can afford. Likewise, that same rich man who can afford a $23 million property "cannot afford" a $35 million house on a more excellent island. So you see? Even a multimillionaire "cannot afford" everything and can appear "broke" or "poor" in relation to a particular house or object of his desire. You are not actually "poor," as you said, except about a specific object of your desire. You are much more than your desires. Remember that.

Stop the poverty mindset from digging deeper into your core, and stop evaluating yourself in relation to the cost of an object. Focusing on the price or cost of a thing you desire cuts you off and disempowers you. Your self-perception becomes entangled with what you lack. When you say, "I cannot afford or am too poor for something," you may resort to borrowing money, taking on unnecessary debts, or otherwise incurring liabilities to match others' standards. That explains why you say, "I'm broke" or "I'm poor." These phrases are expressions of mental negativity in relation to objects you like but cannot afford to buy.

IF MONEY IS THE SOURCE OF EVIL,
THROW IT AWAY

Money is the source of all evils —this is another belief of the mind with mental poverty. Some people associate money with corruption, drugs, and power. If you are rich, people assume you made your money from some shady deals or because of influential connections, luck, or fraudulent activities. People with mental poverty look at rich people with disdain and tend to blame them for their poverty or misery. They even attribute to money all the evils in this world. They cited a biblical basis for their belief. But they refuse to throw their money away.

The Sacred Scriptures say in 1 Timothy, "For the love of money xxx they wandered from their faith." It does not say that money is evil. People have missed the point miserably. They tend to focus only on one word, money, and disregard the true message of the whole. They could have focused on the more positive and promising message in the same Bible about abundance, generous rewards, and parables of talents. Instead, people focus on what makes them poor. They forget that money from the generosity of others builds churches and funds programs to feed and shelter the poor. Money is being used to support various works of charity. Money buys food, medicines, and vaccines. I do not expect to convince you of the virtues of the right money attitude. No, I want to write what I believe. After that, it's up to you what to think.

Yes, money may facilitate some acts of crime. It can motivate people to perform evil deeds. But the poor and the rich alike commit evil acts regardless of money. The evildoer is not money. It is contradictory to aspire for a better life while believing that money is the root of all evil

FINANCIAL LITERACY

Educating yourself on personal finance and other money matters has practical significance. It is a big step forward on your path to financial success. Rich people did not make their millions out of ignorance. On the contrary, they are generally literate on matters of personal finance. Successful people believe in the importance of knowledge. Knowledge feeds the mind. What enriches the mind enriches you.

Federal Reserve Chair Ben Bernanke said people make decisions that ultimately impact the economy. Bernanke said that if people have a better economic and financial understanding, they can make better financial decisions that will lead to better results.

Janet Yellen, another chair of the Federal Reserve, emphasized the importance of people having a basic understanding of economics and developing analytical skills that will be useful in their daily lives.

Financial literacy is basic knowledge or understanding of budgeting, investing, debt management, insurance, financial planning, and other matters that can improve your overall financial strategy and money management.

The rich spend time and money to educate themselves. It explains why reading is a part of their daily activities. They have financial planners or work with financial consultants to educate them in the right direction.

You don't need to be a millionaire to seek advice from these individuals. Find Certified Financial Planners or Financial Advisors in your area. Ensure they are not sales agents. Certified Financial Planners or Advisors work for a fee, But you will always be a winner. It pays to have advisers in your financial journey. Financial literacy levels up the mind. In short, reframe your mind to have a winning mentality and learn from successful people.

Chapter 4

RETIREMENT
WILL CATCH UP TO YOU

"The question isn't at what age I want
to retire; it's at what income."

GEORGE FOREMAN

Let me tell you a job secret they do not usually discuss in the workplace. Do you know that a million dollars are waiting for employees to tap into at the Human Resources Office? As an employee, you have a legal right to claim this money. The guy in your human resources department knows about it. Yes, he can make you a millionaire. That's right: that dude who is not even a millionaire can help you become one. I bet many of you don't believe me. Some of you might want to send me a text message that says, "LOL" (meaning "lots of laughter") or even "&#?@" (meaning "F... you're crazy!").

Well, I can't do anything about your negative mindset. But, I don't see any problem with what I tell you, however unlikely it may appear.

Your propensity to look at the negative side is a genuine concern. Unfortunately, you choose to doubt instead of looking at the possibilities. You decide to dismiss rather than learn what I meant by this bold statement. But even if you don't believe me, let's set this aside for now and dive into a few details you may be interested in.

THERE IS NO WAY UP, BUT IT WON'T LET YOU DOWN: YOUR CAREER

First, look at your healthcare career and ask why you cannot save and how you can do it successfully. They say health care is a dead-end career, that the path to edge up is like going against a funnel turned bottoms up. If you're a respiratory therapist, you will likely do the same at the bedside over the next 20 years. If you were a staff nurse or a physician on staff ten years ago, you are most likely still performing the same routine task of patient care today. Likewise, they say the healthcare field offers poor upward salary potential. To earn more, one must put in more hours at the mill, and any pay increase is a result of either complicated negotiations (through the union) or unilateral management decisions.

But a career in health care is not without its merits. It's important to correct the idea that only working in investment banks or technology companies can lead to high salaries. Entry-level pay for healthcare professionals is not far below that of new employees in technology fields. Moreover, employment in health care means a stable income far from the claws of economic recession; this compensates for any poor upward salary potential.

I remember one early summer day in 2014. We attended an orientation for first-year college applicants at New York University (NYU) in New York for my daughter Katrina. One of the parents asked the university representative, "Which college graduates from the university have the highest employment rate and best pay rate right after graduation?" The answer from the university representative impressed me: "Those would be the graduates from the College of Nursing. One hundred percent are employed immediately after passing the licensure examination." She was pointing to the field of hospitals, not Wall Street.

Likewise, you can pursue your healthcare profession or vocation in a private or government-run facility. If you look hard enough, healthcare facilities still offer a defined benefit pension plan, known as a "pension for life." This type of pension is going extinct today, except in areas of the public sector such as state or local government employment.

REMINDER: YOU EITHER QUIT OR RETIRE

I initially thought about my retirement on the first day I reported for job orientation at the hospital. During the session, someone from human resources explained employee benefits such as tax-deferred accounts. That same day, I signed up for a 403(b). I figured I could retire as a nurse millionaire. After that, what I wanted to have and what I wanted to be—was clear in my mind.

There is nothing immoral about aspiring to be a millionaire nurse. It's the same as attending classes to succeed as a real estate agent while practicing nursing. Again, a nurse pursuing a graduate degree to earn more money as a nurse practitioner is fine. Likewise, there is nothing wrong with a speech therapist who wants to change careers and become a high-priced lawyer in Manhattan. Whatever you want to pursue, keep track of the fact that eventually, no matter what you do, your retirement will catch up to you.

Getting to work is the same as getting closer to retirement, as you routinely get up from bed and drive to work. The moment you start working is the moment you are also beginning to retire. American workers today need to realize it. Instead, they proceed through the grind with short-term goals to cover their short or intermediate needs. The only strategic solution is planting your seed money early, giving it plenty of time to grow into a money tree.

People are typically employed for 25 or 40 years, but even 20 years will be enough only if you save consistently. Every day that you delay shortens your available time by 24 hours. Do not wake up from your sleepwalking to find you are approaching retirement with bags of regrets rather than bags of funds. Sadly, many people run out of time to achieve the financial security they want.

Take note: most workers are unprepared and don't plan on quitting or retiring early. But many are forced to retire, resign, or otherwise quit working due to unavoidable circumstances.

In addition, they often fall from the workforce because of sickness or other reasons beyond their control. So everyone needs a safety net.

On several occasions, I have attended my colleagues' retirement celebrations. In each case, the management handed them a piece of paper or a plaque (or, in one case, nothing) as a token of appreciation for their long dedication and service to the company. Despite the celebratory moment, a closer look at their faces and timid smiles revealed an apprehension for what lies ahead during the retirement years with a small or unsteady stream of income. Many of my colleagues retire with financial insecurities and regrets.

With only a Social Security pension and paltry savings to rely on, no plaque or letter of appreciation could relieve the uncertainty of the absence of a solid retirement account as a safety net in old age. Indeed, any working person has a date with work history: the final date when you stop working.

HAVE A BASELINE

As a healthcare worker, you are familiar with the importance of a baseline to a clinician. A baseline is a reference point that will serve as a basis for comparison. For example, there is a baseline for vital signs. Similarly, there must be a baseline for your money that can serve as the vital signs of your financial standing. In this context, baseline means a financial goal or projected amount of money that serves as a reference point for whether you achieve more than the target or fall below it.

In practical terms, your financial baseline is your target amount of dollars you need to achieve or save at a particular time or age. The numbers won't lie—if the figures you wrote are below or above your financial baseline, you'll know it. For example, at the end of six months, you may want to save $8,000. It is your baseline figure to have in 6 months. It can also be an amount you wish to have at a certain age— for example, having $350,000 at the age of 45. If you save more than that amount upon reaching the specific age or time, then you did a good job.

I encourage you to use "one million dollars" as the baseline for your long-term goal. Then, whenever you achieve that one million dollars, whether that's age 45, 50, or 60, you will have that appreciative feeling of being financially successful. You can pat yourself on the back in front of a mirror and say, "Ah, here is a millionaire healthcare worker." And you will have a special sense of pride that you—yes, you—have joined the rank of millionaires! (After all, who has to know you have "only" one or two million? It still counts.)

Spectrem Group's Market Insight Report for 2020 mentioned that only about 12 million American household millionaires (excluding their equity in their primary residence). That is about 12 million out of roughly 129 million American households in 2020.[2] On the other hand, according to Credit Suisse Global Wealth Report 2020, there are about 20.27 million millionaires in the USA out of the entire 250 million adult population. About 20% of US millionaires inherited their wealth.[3] You can feel pride when joining their rank through determination and effort.

Again, write a realistically bigger goal just as you want a larger amount of financial baseline. Be confident. Remember those first few checks you received back when you first started working? At the beginning of your financial journey, it will be challenging to raise even the first $10,000, especially if you are fresh from college. The same is true with the first $100,000. I remember how difficult and daunting it was to raise my first $100,000. There were many leaps and bounds, and it was a complicated journey. But the experience taught me that the path kept getting easier after the first $10,000 or after the first $100,000, and after every other milestone. The drive I took to reach the next one kept getting shorter.

How can this be? You and your money are already working together to build more value.

---

2   Spectrem Group, "Coronavirus Reduces Millionaire Count."
3   Shorrocks, Davies, and Lluberas, "The Global Wealth Report 2020."

As time went on, you became more innovative. You make better choices and decisions. You learned what expenses and financial mistakes to avoid. You acquired new money-saving skills and insight. So you see: you can unlock your millionaire potential. Be confident enough to write a bigger goal. Don't hesitate to set a bigger financial baseline. Financial success is not only the addition of dollars and figures; it involves handling money skills, financial knowledge, better choices and decisions, sound strategies, and experiences.

SECURE YOUR RETIREMENT

On a positive note, 25 years or even 20 years away from retirement is an excellent stretch to achieve financial security, provided you consistently set aside money in a tax-sheltered account. It does not matter how much you earn when you have a long period to save. They don't make much difference— your secret weapon is time, and your strategy is wise management of what you can set aside. Time is continuity and progression. An hour is just a unit or measure of time. The power of compounding works best with time.

Choose to have a larger money goal for your retirement fund. You will likely have a sizable fund even if you fail to reach your goal. If others aspire to get promotions, what is wrong with aspiring to be a multimillionaire retiree instead? We are not used to hearing in our workplaces or even social gatherings that someone is working toward becoming a millionaire. The topic seems taboo—but it is acceptable to discuss a pay increase or a promotion. It is the prevailing state of mind for many working American men and women.

That's why such a significant number of people retire from work with such dismal savings. But what if 99.9% of us changed the way we think?

THE GEM IS IN YOUR HR DEPARTMENT

At the start of this chapter, I told you that the HR guy, who is not a millionaire, can help you become one. You might have been skeptical about that assertion. But wait—don't run to your human resources department just yet. There's a crucial factor to consider: knowing how to ask the right question. Additionally, chances are HR may not be equipped to provide the suitable response to your question.

Here is what I meant to tell you. First, as a freshly employed healthcare worker, your HR department staff should have been your first stop because your HR is the steward of a depository of knowledge and information about your employee benefits.

The essential information you need from your HR guy is the information you need that has a bearing on your employment decision to stay or leave the company. What does the company offer to secure your well-being regarding health and financial benefits? How long are these benefits vested, and what is the retirement formula for calculating your pension if offered? Are your health benefits reasonably priced and appropriate for your family? Ask the HR guy to explain the available 401(k), 403(b), or 457(b) program(s) and assist you in signing up for one. How much does the company give as a matching contribution toward your retirement? Does it offer any incentives if you want to pursue higher education? These are the most important benefits. The rest are mere icing on the cake.

IS YOUR PAY OR BENEFITS WORTH IT?

As a healthcare employee, you will find a range of employers offering varying pay rates, work incentives, and benefits. Some offer nothing but a toxic workplace. You might find yourself at the same employer for 5, 10, or 25 years. Spending even one year with an employer with inadequate benefits can be a waste of your time. Your valuable clinical experience, talents, and skills deserve to be recognized and commensurately compensated.

Only when you know about these benefits can you ask yourself if it is worth staying with this company or employer—or if it is only prepared to offer you a piece of candy and a whistle at the end of your long career. In any case, you can bring your talents, clinical skills, and experience elsewhere. These few pieces of information are not to be taken for granted. It is your life: you are spending your earning years with your employer. You cannot return the time you gave to your company which provides you with lousy benefits. Make sure that you are compensated at the end. Believe me. I have met several healthcare workers who regretted staying in the same place until the end of their careers because they "were happy and knew everybody" while working there. Did you try to work in other places where you have a problem knowing everyone and not being happy?

Here is what I meant when I told you that the HR guy could make a big difference in your life; he can introduce you to all the benefits your employer offers. Most specifically, he can help you sign up for a retirement account. The power of tax-free compounding returns will supercharge your money and your company-matched contribution (if there is any) to make you a millionaire healthcare worker. Over time, if you start early, your initial balance can reach a million dollars. See? The dude in HR can make you a millionaire.

Ask your colleagues if they have ever heard of saving taxes with an FSA or HSA. Most of them will give you a negative answer, or they may say they've heard of them but don't understand what an FSA or HSA can do for them. Do you know what an FSA or HSA is? No? If not, there may be two reasons. One: you did not ask or did not hear it mentioned. Two: you were falling asleep when an HR staff mentioned them in the orientation meeting session—or, just as likely, the HR person was also drowsy to talk about FSA or HSA. WAKE UP HR STAFF: DO YOUR WORKERS A FAVOR

On a side note, most Human Resources departments need to improve at explaining and promoting their 401(k) s, 403(b)s, and other company benefits. HR staff needs to be proactive in explaining company benefits to all company employees.

Employees have a legal and vested right to know what they are entitled to as company employees.

As a healthcare worker, your time is tight, and you live a busy life. Even so, don't ever think you are wasting time by trying to learn about personal finance or get better at handling your money. The time you spend educating your-self about managing your dough is just as important as the time you spend making it. Remember, you build one million dollars on additions. So knowledge is always an addition.

Chapter 5

OPPORTUNITY COST AND BETTER CHOICES

"There is an opportunity cost for everything we do. That is why we must have the awareness to ensure that what we are pursuing is what we value. Because the pursuit leaves countless lost opportunities in its wake. We choose one experience at the sacrifice of all other experiences."

CHRIS MATAKAS, THE TAO OF JIU JITSU

One irony of human anatomy is that man has two hands and two feet but cannot have two things or in two places at the same time— all the time. So you and I have to make decisions or choices. When we choose one option over the others, any value or benefits we can derive from those we have rejected—including any opportunity that may have arisen from or been brought by those we rejected—are gone forever. These benefits are what we have traded away. That is our payment for declining or leaving one thing in favor of another. It is the cost we paid for the opportunity to choose one over the other. It is an opportunity cost.

This chapter examines the variables in decision-making and deals with the importance of understanding the concept of opportunity cost to identify and decide on our best choices.

This practical concept in economics and business operations applies to everyday financial and personal affairs. To reiterate, opportunity cost stands as your most strategic financial tool—an essential skill akin to a trade that you must possess.

DECISION AND CHOICES

Our choices and decisions today, if taken collectively with those we've made in the past, telegraph the future. Our choices and decisions concerning critical and minor issues change and define our lives.

Who we are and what will become of us are impacted by what appears to be a routine or pattern of small daily decisions. We all pay the price for it and are delighted by the consequences of our decisions or choices. However, we pay the opportunity cost to enjoy the possible benefits or gains from the other path not taken.

We all make choices and decisions all the time. Even when you didn't lift a finger, you still made a choice: you made a choice not to lift your finger. But, simultaneously, you paid the cost of the opportunities you might have had if you had done something different. That is where the problem lies. We often make choices or decisions by considering the instant benefits and attractiveness of the glass that holds the water, but we need to take steps further down the road to discover the brooks where the water flows. Our failure to decide to walk further down and find the streams is a lost opportunity with a cost, especially when we cannot go back to it.

Our decision-making process is more straightforward when confronted with options or choices with obviously unequal value. In these cases, we only need to compare the value, benefits, cost basis, and advantages of one option over the benefits offered by the alternatives, and then we decide. However, in some instances, it is challenging to select one from the options before us: it prompts us to choose on the spot—and our choice or decision turns out to be costly or disadvantageous compared to another we initially rejected. Because our frame of mind is drawn to the obvious and immediate, we fail to look at the latent value and benefits of the other option. It is the cost of opportunity.

Unfortunately, as consumers, we do not weigh our choices enough, especially when shopping in the grocery store or mall. Therefore, we must pay attention to the opportunity costs that can impact our finances over time.

OPPORTUNITY COST: A CASE STUDY

Donald is a physical therapist at Western Hospital. He wants to purchase a car for around $26,500 on a five-year loan term. He considers a Toyota RAV4 and a Honda CR-V, which have comparable safety and convenient features. Donald thinks that both cars are excellent and meet his driving requirements. But the RAV4 has a ticket price of $21,000 at 2.75% interest, while the CR-V's price is $20,690 at 0% interest with a required $3,600 down (without a down payment, the interest rate is 3.10%). Donald likes the color of the Honda CR-V; prompted by the sales agent, he decides to come up with the $3,600 down payment to avail himself of the 0% interest.

Question: How would you decide if you were in Donald's shoes?

Answer: First, we must identify this case's most important aspects. Let us consider the price, the interest rate, and the outright $3,600 cash requirement if Donald decides he wants the 0% interest. He can also choose a car loan at 3.10% interest.

On the other hand, if Donald puts down $3,600 toward either car, he loses the opportunity to use that cash for other purposes. If he didn't pay a downpayment for a car, he could use that money to pay off a credit card that charges as much as 20% (compared to Honda's 3.10%). He could use the $3,600 to max out his 401(k) contribution, or it could be set aside in a Roth IRA to grow by 7% to 9% annually. These are just a few examples of the costs of trading the opportunity to use that $3,600 to get the vehicle he wants at 0% interest.

OPPORTUNITY COST

Opportunity cost is an important financial tool to help us arrive at a financially favorable decision or choice by assessing the other options or alternatives in our day-to-day lives.

It involves looking at the benefits, value, cost, profitability, and opportunities arising from the possibility we might reject. Once we decide to reject or give up one option in favor of another, our decision's actual cost or price is the loss of the latent opportunity, value, and benefits from that alternative we rejected.

The opportunity cost is the imaginary cost or conceptual price we pay for trading one thing over another. Determining our opportunity cost means looking not only at one choice's instant benefits but also at its long-term value and the possible opportunities that could have arisen from the choice we are trading away. Opportunity cost is an imaginary cost of what we reject whenever we choose a different alternative. This concept of opportunity cost may seem simple—until we find ourselves in a complicated situation that calls for a hard decision.

Here's an example: Nurse John wants to pursue graduate studies to become a nurse practitioner, but he would need to pay $45,000 for the two-year program. So if he decides to go back to school, the following are the trade-offs:

→ John will shell out $45,000 for tuition, books, and other school fees. He will either pay for this in cash or take out a loan with interest.

→ John will lose the opportunity to use that $45,000 for other gainful purposes, such as investing it, instead of using the money to pay for school.

→ John will devote time to his commute and studies that could be spent with his family.

→ John will have less time and opportunity to earn overtime pay or extra work shifts as he will be busy with studies, commuting, research, and other school-related activities.

If John chooses not to go to graduate school, the opportunity cost or trade-off are the following:

→ John will miss out on the earning potential of a nurse practitioner.

→ John will lose the career opportunities that may come from graduate studies.

$\rightarrow$ John will not experience the personal satisfaction of attaining his graduate degree.

The most important questions are: How much does it cost you to lose or miss out on career opportunities that may arise as a Nurse Practitioner, and how much, in terms of the earning potential, will you give up? What is the value of giving up your sense of satisfaction or fulfilling your dream?

SUMMARY

What will it cost you to do or choose this and not that? Opportunity cost is the "imaginary cost" of the thing you have not selected or rejected. It is the hypothetical cost you paid for choosing A and rejecting B. It is the value of what you gave up or traded away when you chose one over other choices. This cost can be an actual price or value or the advantages or opportunities that might have come from the options or alternatives you rejected. Because you prefer or like what you decided on.

Therefore, when we make decisions or choices, we must take a more expansive view of our options by having a long-term outlook. We should execute our decisions only after looking at the long-term consequences and considering the probable outcome rather than deciding on a short-term basis with a small frame of mind. Opportunity cost impacts our careers, money, relationships, and all other aspects of our lives. We can make consequential decisions that lead to better outcomes by considering and applying the concept of the opportunity cost at every turn.

Chapter 6

SAVE MONEY AND INVEST WHAT YOU SAVE

"The poor save. The rich don't save."

WARREN BUFFETT

Many healthcare workers are apprehensive and even distrustful when they hear the word invest or investment. They associate these words with some speculative gambling or risky game of chance. As a consequence, they are afraid to invest. Instead, they consider banks and local credit unions safe places to put their money. They even think tax-deferred accounts are "scary" investments because of stock market gyrations. So they opt to "fatten" their piggy banks through CDs or money market accounts despite knowing that banks and local credit unions pay a pathetic 1.0% to 1.5% annual interest.

Don't get me wrong. Banks and credit unions generate jobs for the community and provide funds for local businesses. But regarding your financial well-being, bank deposits are poor choices for long-term investment goals. As Warren Buffett said, "The poor save. The rich don't save." That's because the rich invest their money.

It's high time to discard your misconceptions about investments. Investing doesn't have to be scary. Change your mindset! Save to invest, invest to save. There are vehicles of investment with varying degrees of risk of loss. Still, the risk is minimized when investing for the long term to secure your retirement. So set aside money for investment and make it part of your long-term financial planning.

DON'T BE A CUSTOMER—OWN THE COMPANY

Take note of this: you like your bank and you have been using the products of certain companies. These products and services make your life convenient and caffeine-filled. For example, you love to drink coffee every morning from Starbucks. Likewise, you and your family buy a lot of stuff from Costco and Amazon from the comfort of your home. You are captivated by Netflix and Disney movies and you cannot leave the house without your Apple devices. Meanwhile, your money is safely parked in a bank account. But have you ever thought of becoming a part owner or stockholder of your bank, Netflix, Starbucks, Apple, McDonald's, or any other companies you and your family have patronized for years?

How? Invest. That's right—it's time to invest. So don't be afraid of the word invest. I'm about to share the vehicles of investments that will allow you to grow your money, especially if time is on your side.

SHARES OF STOCKS

A stock represents ownership or equity in a company. For example, when you buy shares of stock of your bank, your favorite coffee, Starbucks, or Amazon, you invest in these companies and acquire equity or you become an owner in proportion to your shares. You are a stockholder or shareholder of the company regardless of how many shares you own in that company (See Chapter 14).

As a part owner of the bank, for example, you also share in the bank's profit as dividends. Your profit (dividends) from the bank will probably be higher than the interest on your deposit. Some companies give 3 to 5% in dividends compared to the 1.5% to 2% bank interest on your money in the bank.

You might ask about the risk. Yes, there is some risk. But think about this: If you can trust your bank to hold on to your hard-earned money, why wouldn't you want to become a bank owner?

J.B. Maverick, writing for Investopedia.com in February 2020, reported: "From 1926 to 2018, the average annual return of the S&P 500 is approximately 10% to 11%. From January 2005 to December 2019, the average annual return is 10.45%."[4] There is no way your favorite bank or credit union can pay interest on your deposit that will beat those stock market returns.

Likewise, stocks are some of the most convenient investment vehicles compared to other investment forms like real estate. Stocks require less money or capital to start investing.

You can open an account with a stockbroker for a minimum of $500. You can ask your bank to transfer your money directly into an investment or brokerage account. To start,

---

4   Investopedia, "J.B. Maverick."

you can buy stocks of just two or three companies. You can also start with mutual funds.

To appreciate the growth of your investments, the money you put toward stocks or mutual funds must be money you will not need or use for at least three years. (If you're worried about keeping your money in one place for three or more years, don't be. Hasn't the money you've deposited in the bank been sitting there for years?)

Let me recall a time in 2009. I had a coworker named Michelle, an RN. Michelle was in her mid-thirties. Once, during our downtime—when patients were quiet, and every-thing was slow in the unit—we talked about how to send our kids to college. I remember very well that, at the time, I told her to buy shares of Bank of America (BAC). At that time, the share was trading at about $3, and some change. I told Michelle that BAC's stocks and dividends could finance her youngest child's college education. That was in 2009.

Fast forward to February 2022, the share of BAC was trading at more than $48 per share. The capital gains are enough to finance Michelle's daughter's college tuition fees at the local community college. Of course, that assumes Michelle bought at least 2,000 shares, which she could have easily. By the way, Bank of America also gives roughly 4% dividends per share, more than the 2% interest it gives on deposits. If the dividends are used to buy additional shares, the original shares, plus those additional shares, will give a compounded income.

With those BAC shares, Michelle's daughter could have registered in the community college as a full scholar of the Bank of A. And when she graduates in four years, she will still have enough money to buy a new car or start a new investment.

MUTUAL FUNDS

A mutual fund is a pool of money that is contributed by investors and managed by investment professionals. Mutual funds can be either Stock Mutual Funds, Bond Funds, or both, depending on where the money is invested. If invested only in stocks or more concentrated into stocks than bonds, it is called a Stock Mutual Fund. It is called Bond Fund when it is concentrated in bonds. Balance Fund is when the fund invests or the money is put 50% into the bonds and 50% into the stocks, but variations may be allowed. The money in the fund or pool is invested in various companies.

As an investor in the mutual fund, you have ownership in the fund in proportion to the number of your shares. Unlike buying individual stocks of a particular company—for example, TESLA AMAZON or COSTCO —with a mutual fund, your investment money bought various companies, including international companies. That is called diversification. Your risk is lower than if you had invested in an individual company's stock (see Chapter 16 for more discussion).

BONDS

Another vehicle of investment where you can park your money is a bond or bond fund. A bond is an instrument of indebtedness issued by a private company, the sovereign government, or a city, state, or government agency. When you invest in bonds or bond funds, you lend money to the company, state, or government agency that issued the bonds. As a result, you receive a regular interest payment from the borrower.

When you purchase bonds, you do not become a part owner or owner of the company but rather a lender. On the other hand, by investing in stock, you own equity or ownership in the company in proportion to your shares, so you share in the company's profit.

Since 1926, the average yearly bond return has been about 5 to 6%. As a result, bonds are more stable and have a lower risk exposure than stocks (see Chapter 15 for more discussion).

BOND FUNDS

A Bond Fund is like a mutual fund. The bond fund is also a pool of investors' money managed by investment professionals. The fund is invested in various bonds issued by companies and government entities. Investing in bonds or bond funds does not require much start-up money. You can start with a minimum of $500 or less. It is easy, convenient, and less risky than investing in stocks or stock mutual funds (that only invest in stocks). However, the return is lower than stocks. According to a leading investment research firm, Morningstar, long-term government bonds have returned roughly 6 to 7% over the last 30 years.

Like any investment, bonds or bond funds involve risk. One is a credit risk, meaning that there is a danger that a private corporation cannot pay because its business slows down or that the city, state, or government agency fails to generate the necessary income to pay its obligations. Another risk is a premature call of the bond. It is when the company or government pays the bonds before maturity. Maturity is the time fixed for the borrower to pay the debt or the bonds and interest. A rising interest rate affects bonds, which lose value when the interest rate increases.

REIT

REIT stands for real estate investment trust, another investment vehicle providing diversification. Like a mutual fund, a REIT is a pool of professionally managed money from investors. However, the money is invested in real estate instead of stocks or bonds. It does not invest in the physical buildings or the actual houses. Instead, you invest in the companies engaged in the real estate business. The REIT invests in various income-producing real estate properties. Many financial experts consider REITs to be substitute investments for actual physical properties.

Tara Mastroeni, writing for Business Insider, stated that REITs allow people to invest in real estate without having to buy or manage any property. When investing in REITs, you invest in an extensive account of properties within the REIT portfolio, such as hotels, apartments, and shopping centers.[5] The educational website of the US Securities and Exchange Commission, investor.gov, explains that a REIT is a company that owns and operates an income-producing real estate or related real property. These may include office buildings, shopping malls, apartments, hotels, resorts, warehouses, and mortgages.

---

5   Mastroeni, "REITs Are a Way to Own Real Estate without Becoming a Landlord—Here's How They Work, How to Invest, and the Different Kinds to Invest In."

REIT companies do not develop or construct buildings or houses or any other real estate properties to resell them; they buy these buildings and may even develop real estate properties to operate them as a form of investment.[6]

In the article "Investing in REIT 101: Pros and Cons," the author, Matthew Frankel, CFP, says that REIT distributes high dividends and offers diversification to investors. REITs are also liquid investments. However, buying and selling real estate properties consumes more time than other real estate investments. In addition, complying with regulations requires the coordinated assistance of others, such as real estate agents, notaries, and mortgage brokers.[7]

Like any form of investment, REITs are sensitive to rising interest rates. As a result, this type of investment is taxed at a higher rate than stocks or mutual funds, which is why various sources recommend investing in REITs through tax-deferred retirement accounts.

529 B COLLEGE SAVINGS PLAN

You can also put money in a 529b for your child's college expenses. In some states, your contribution to 529b is tax deductible. The money grows tax-free. When you withdraw the money for qualified expenses like books, tuition fees, a computer, and other school-related items, all the funds you withdraw are tax-free (see Chapter 21 for more information).

---

6   U.S. Securities and Exchange Commission, "Real Estate Investment Trusts (REITs)."

7   Frankel, "Investing in REITs 101: The Pros and Cons."

YOUR EMPLOYER'S RETIREMENT ACCOUNTS

Another vehicle you can ride into the stock and bond market is your employer-sponsored 401(k), 403(b), or 457(b). For health workers with a long-term goal, contributing to a retirement account where your employer matches your contribution is the best strategy for becoming a millionaire or securing your retirement.

Employers usually match your contribution to your retire-ment account, a dollar for every dollar you contribute, up to as much as 3 or 5% of the money you set aside. That is a free flow of money that, together with your contribution, earns a compounded return for years (see Chapters 17 &18). And if free money from your employer wasn't enough to take advan-tage of these accounts, your contribution to this account is tax deductible. It means that your contribution can lower your tax base, thus lowering your tax liability.

The higher your contribution, the more it can lower your taxes. It is one of those secret strategies that even aver-age earners can use to make their money work overtime to retire a millionaire or with a stash of million dollars. This is what rich people meant when they said they don't save but they invest. Do not be afraid to invest.

TAX RATE COMPARISON: ORDINARY INCOME VS. CAPITAL GAINS

You've heard people complain about paying high taxes. I've heard a lot of complaints from my coworkers. They grumble that so much money has already been taken from them every payday, as reflected in their W-2s. However, they still pay more come April 15. And it's true. Because your income from work is an ordinary income subject to a higher rate of taxes. Do you ever look at your taxes and wonder what happened to all that extra overtime pay? Instead of getting you more money, your additional income slumps you up to a higher tax bracket.

As the tax filing deadline approaches, do you wonder why the other guy in the corner hums a happy tune while you scramble to find the money to pay the IRS? Here is the difference between you and your colleague.

You and your spouse are joint filers. You figured out that your combined income from regular work is $130,000. You also noted that you made an additional $25,000 from working overtime. So your gross income for the year is $155,000. But you realize you have an extra $2,000 from bank interest, bringing you and your husband's total income to $157,000. So after taking out your 2022 standard deduction of $25,900, your taxable income is $131,100 —which catapulted you into a 24% tax rate for the 2022 federal tax. Now you understand why so many people complain about the US tax system.

In contrast, your colleague Peter Wise, a respiratory therapist, and his wife (working in an admitting Unit) have a combined work income of $135,000. But instead of working overtime, Peter goes fishing on his off days. To supplement his income, he sold his stock investments after one year for a gain of $25,000. Peter and his wife have contributed $37,000 to their 401(k)s and $3,500 to their health savings account (HSA). So, after deducting their combined 401(k) contributions of $37,000, their standard federal deduction of $25,900, and the $3,500 to their HSA, the couple's taxable work income is $68,600. The $25,000 capital gain or profit from selling stocks is not part of an ordinary income. It is excluded. Do you know what the Wise couple's 2022 federal tax rate is? About 12% tax for their work income compared to your 24% tax rate. How about Peter's $25,000 profit from selling his stocks? For 2022, Peter Wise will pay roughly 15% capital gain tax (Not an ordinary income tax rate), compared to your 24% tax rate on the $25,000 extra income from overtime shifts. The average tax burden of healthcare workers is a whopping 22%. That rate is applied to all your regular and overtime pay.

Billionaire investor Warren Buffett admitted that his secretary, Debbie Bosanek, paid higher taxes than him. So what we read and hear is true: the rich are getting richer and paying lower taxes than the working middle class. Compare the stark contrast between the seemingly oppressive tax rate of an ordinary income tax and the capital gains tax for income from long-term investments of at least one year.

Here is the 2023 CAPITAL GAINS TAX table for your examination:

Single Filers With Taxable Income of…	Married Joint Filers With Taxable Income of…	Married Couples Filing Separately With Taxable Income of…	Heads of Households With Taxable Income of…	Pay a Long-Term Capital Gains Tax Rate of…
$0 to $44,625	$0 to $89,250	$0 to $44,625	$0 to $59,750	0%
$44,626 to $492,300	$89,251 to $553,850	$44,626 to $276,900	$59,751 to $523,050	15%
Over $492,300	Over $553,850	Over $276,900	Over $523,050	20%

LOOK at the 2023 ORDINARY INCOME TAX RATE for your consideration:

Rate	For Single Individuals, Taxable Income Over	For Married Couples Filing Jointly, Taxable Income Over	For Heads of Households, Taxable Income Over
10%	Up to $11,000	Up to $22,000	Up to $15,700
12%	$11,000	$22,000	$15,700
22%	$44,725	$89,450	$59,850
24%	$95,375	$190,750	$95,350
32%	$182,100	$364,200	$182,100
35%	$231,250	$462,500	$231,250
37%	$578,125	$693,750	$578,100

Did you notice the huge difference? Consider this—earning money doesn't necessarily mean working harder for more money. Instead, it's letting your money work to bring you more money. This is known as passive income, meaning that your money or investments do the money-making without you having to play an active role. And that's not all; the most advantageous aspect is paying a tax rate of 0% and 15% (depending on your filing status), a stark contrast to the 22% to 32% that burdens the working class. This information may make you scream, "That's so unfair!" But should blame be placed on those who dared to take risks and invested their money, or is the system the real issue?

Just look at these common reactions people have when they hear about investments:

→   "No, stocks aren't for me; my neighbor lost a lot of money in a retirement account invested in stocks."

→   "A certificate of deposit is best for me. I know I won't lose anything in the bank."

→   "The bank is a safe place to save money."

→   "Stocks are just a form of gambling."

The American financial system is meant for risk-takers and investors, large and small. America provides the world's best playground for entrepreneurs and people who invest. The lower tax rate on capital gains rewards people who take risks and invest their money for the long haul. The investors and risk-takers deserve a lower tax rate, not the passive and fearful ones. Yes, it may seem unfair. But the reality is that investors expose their capital to the market forces with all their attendant risks. Likewise, entrepreneurs take more significant financial risks than those who are employed. That is because they have so much to lose.

That is one of the secrets of how ordinary people become millionaires: they have the mental stamina to assume risk. So don't be afraid of the word invest. Think of what Robert G. Allen once said: "How many millionaires do you know who have become wealthy by investing in a savings account? I rest my case."

Chapter 7

LET YOUR MIND TRANSCEND RISK

"If you think something is important enough, you should try. Even if the probable outcome is a failure."

ELON MUSK

This chapter emphasizes the value of risk assessment and risk-taking concerning our pursuit of success, especially in personal finance. Your money will not grow or work for you if you only think about safety and fear of risk. Even in your profession or career, you will only advance if you leave your comfort zone. You will be stuck in that slow traffic if you are not willing to take what might be an unfamiliar route,

The ability to take risks is an expression of our faith and self-affirmation. It manifests our confidence in our capacity and a belief that our undertaking will have a better outcome than the cost. Nothing worthwhile comes easy.

Millionaires took some risks to make their money. If you want to make more than what your bank gives on your deposit, you must invest that money by taking some risk. Investing your money comes with risk, as do many other everyday transactions. For example, owning real estate comes with risk. Your money in a bank deposit has a risk: it will lose value from inflation. Even buying your own house has financial consequences. The value of your home will go down significantly. Risk is always there. If you don't want to take the risk, don't expect the world to show the opportunity to open up.

I admire risk-takers. They are strong people with human stories that can make you wonder how they overcame many pains and emerged unbroken. But while many were rewarded for their risks, many other risk-takers have yet to succeed. Whether they failed or succeeded, they deserve our admiration for taking a chance many others did not have the guts to take.

KNOW THE RISK TO SUCCEED

Financial experts advise us to take risks to make money. They say the greater the risk, the greater the gains. We heard that to succeed; we need to take risks. No guts, no glory. But they forgot to tell us one essential element that will change the game: you must know about the risks involved before taking them. It amounts to one single word: Know the risk you are getting into.

Our fear lies in the fact that we do not know something. The trouble lies in uncertainty. So let me tell you. Reverse it. Get to know the basics about the thing. Revisit it. Rethink about it. Have some knowledge or idea about the risk, then take the chance to succeed. All the rest, your mind is powerful enough to transcend risks and overcome them.

What does risk-taking have to do with the process of achieving financial success? First, as I've mentioned elsewhere, any investment involves risks. That risk comes with the very nature of the activity or undertaking itself. The risk may also arise from other variables, directly or indirectly, related or unrelated to your undertaking or act.

When you invest in stocks or mutual funds, for example, you accept the risk that a company will fail to meet its projected revenue, and the value of its shares will plummet. Fortuitous events can adversely affect the company's operations. Even if a company is profitable and doing well, a negative perception of the company among investors is a risk that has the potential to lower the value of the company. Yes, there are always risks. But what is the worst that can happen, and what is its probability? Weigh the benefits and rewards versus the likelihood of the risk occurring. If you do not know the risk, have someone from the field guide you or assess the dangers.

FACES AND MANIFESTATIONS OF RISK

Risks have different faces and expressions. In the face of threat or danger, you can consider risk as either malignant or benign depending on how you size it up. You can make the risk uglier or diminish it to annoyance by how you appraise it. You give a face to the risk. Do you look at yourself in the mirror and see the apprehensive or even frightened expression of a person too fearful of taking that first step outside his comfort zone? Study the risk, know it, and you will tame it.

Most risks depend on you, not the activity or transaction you want to engage in. Don't get me wrong; apprehension is a normal reaction to accepting risk. But it should not stop you. Instead, it should prompt you to study the threat, familiarize yourself with it, calculate, plan, and seek sound advice.

THE GREATER RISK IS YOU

We often discover that the greater risk is ourselves because we are afraid to take risks. At times, we are too fearful of confronting our feelings of fear: the more significant and bolder your undertaking, the greater the corresponding fear of risk.

Risk can also mean a potential loss of money as an investment. As with sports and other high-stakes physical competitions, risks can be physical harm, injury, or loss. The potential consequences of taking a stand for a cause or moral position on an issue can be a profound risk. Risk can mean legal liability, job loss, shame, dishonor, or inconveniences from putting one's foot forward. Risk can be imaginary or real. Ask yourself: Will the risk far outweigh the benefits of taking a position or stand? Is the apprehension of danger any riskier than not taking the risk?

HOW MILLIONAIRES LOOK AT RISK

In the book Everyday Millionaires: How Ordinary People Built Extraordinary Wealth—and How You Can Too, the author, Chris Hogan, wrote that based on his studies of millionaires in the US, when it comes to risk, "Millionaires understand that risk is something to be managed, not avoided. They tread carefully, weigh the risk and potential reward, and then move forward cautiously and confidently, knowing their success is in their own hands."[8]

In his book, The Top 10 Distinctions between Millionaires and the Middle Class, Keith Cameron Smith wrote: "While

8   Hogan, *Everyday Millionaires.*

middle-class people are often content to stay in their lane, millionaires strive to move out of theirs. Put another way; the middle class lives in fear of risking too much, while millionaires know when to go for it. Millionaires overcome fear, and the middle class submits to it." And what is responsible for this vastly different approach to risk? Smith further wrote: "Millionaires overcome fear with knowledge. Millionaires educate themselves before taking risks, and then they consider the consequences of failing."

FOCUS ON REWARDS, NOT JUST RISK

I was prompted to write this chapter after I met one young woman on an EVA Air flight in August 2019. Her name was Janice Lang from Houston, Texas, she was around 35 years old. We were on our way to Taipei from Los Angeles, California. Janice was at the plane's tail end, drinking coffee and chatting with a flight attendant. She said she just wanted to stretch, and I was engaged in my habit of walking around inside the plane during a long flight when I had the chance to meet with Janice.

During our conversation, I learned that this young woman owns a business franchise in Houston, Texas. She also told me she has two residential houses and a small commercial building. She used to work as a programmer in a tech company in Houston, but business caught her fascination. When I expressed my admiration and praised her achievements at such an early age, while so many others had not taken an initial step, she got fired up and became even more vocal about how she had made it.

She told me, "I used my savings for a down payment on a small house. I'm renting that out. After I left my company, I bought another small residential house and rented that out, too." She continued, "It's OK to consult people and ask them what you should do and the risks. But ultimately, the risk is just in mind. When you focus on risk, your mind focuses only on the risk, and you forget the bigger returns. Many people only focus on the risk and fail to see the greater risk to themselves for not taking the necessary risk to move up. America is good for people who want to take risks." (I could only respond: "God bless America!")

Ms. Lang added that most of the time, the foreseeable risks she planned for were different from the risks that came to pass. She told me about her partnership with a friend to buy a commercial property. After all the time wasted and money spent on legal and financial consultations, her friend left the partnership and refused to pay her share of the expenses. This particular risk was not foreseeable—but Ms. Lang persevered. Now it's her three-story building.

People often have unfounded fears and refuse to take risks. People always want to be correct and do the right thing, treating every mistake as a failure. People cannot handle rejection and denial. Sure, those things hurt—but nothing is more painful than letting fear prevent you from trying.

Let me end this chapter with a reminder from the champion:

"Any fear is an illusion. You think something is standing in your way, but nothing is there. What is there is an opportunity to do your best and gain some success."

—Michael Jordan, NBA

Chapter 8

TIME AND MONEY

"A simple fact that is hard to learn is that the time
to save money is when you have some."

JOE MOORE

So you have reached this far in this book. It means you take a serious interest in making a difference in your financial life. You can look at yourself in the mirror and tell yourself, "I am a millionaire in the making." Congratulations!

Have you ever wondered how time relates to your money or financial goals? Did you ever think about that for a moment?

TEMPUS FUGIT

Tempus fugit is a Latin phrase meaning "time flies." Don't ever think the future is far away. Time flies and never returns. One day lost is your 24 hours lost. A day you missed to start securing your future is a long time wasted. You cannot bring back the wasted time. You cannot buy time with money. So let us learn from the past and plan for the future.

Everything you do today, whatever you plan, and whatever choices you make at present have bearings in the future. Twenty-five or 30 years from now is a long time, but it will be here before you know it with all the baggage of what you have today. As mentioned, time can make a big difference in what you have today and what you will have in the future. Time flies.

RETIREMENT: A FUTURE TENSE

You start to retire on the first day you start working. Every day you go to work is one day you get closer to retirement. Retirement is a future event. When discussing retirement, you discuss a future event that will occur at a foreseeable time in reference to your age. So one can say, "I will retire in 5 years "or "10 more years. "The person is saying that by making his present age the reference point to the future event. When you talk of the "future," you talk about the period between this present time and that foreseeable time when you expect something to take place.

The time between the present and the future is the measure of time that you can accomplish, achieve something or fail or do nothing at all. A happy retirement is not only about health; it's about having finances to spend on what you want to enjoy.

RELATIONSHIP BETWEEN TIME AND MONEY

You heard many times that "Time is money. "But you seldom heard somebody saying that money is time. You cannot bring back the time you lost. Your money cannot buy time or use it to extend time. But time can get back the money or even bring back more than what you lost.

For example, if you refuse a job offer that pays $15 more than what you presently earn per hour, what you actually refused or lost is the $15.00 an hour difference or the opportunity to make that money. However, in case another option comes again, and you decide to take a job offer that pays $15 or $18 more than your current hourly pay, in that case, you are just given a new opportunity to earn the money you forgo but not the time.

Your money is worth more now than the same sum in the future. Because you can use now the money or it has time to grow more. That is the relationship between time and money.

Based on studies by Fidelity Investment, if a 25-year-old worker invests $5,500 yearly ($458.33 per month) for only ten years until the age of 35 and stops investing at that age, they will have $620,000 at age 65. Fidelity further said that if that same person waited for ten years, started investing at age 35, and continued investing $5,500 every year for 30 years, he would have only $556,000 at age 65. Time made the difference.

Furthermore, a 25-year-old worker with less money, who invests $300 every month in a mutual fund earning an annual 10% compound interest (based on the historical rate of return of the stock market), will have $1,027,768 at age 65. Compare this with a worker with $30,000 in savings who began investing at age 40; he will need to invest $1,200 a month at the same 10% compound interest to have $1,070,609 at age 65. So, again, time made the difference.

Do you remember the story of Ms. Sherrel, the Nursing Assistant, mentioned in Chapter 2? She started working in a nursing facility when she was only 23 years old and stayed there for 12 years until she left when she was 35. If she had only known of her employer's 401(k) and contributed at least $230 to that retirement account every two weeks for ten years, based on an average 10% annual return of S&P 500 stocks, she would likely have more than half a million dollars at age 65. For Ms. Sherrel, that time between age 23 (when she started working in the facility) and age 35 (when she left) determines what she would have in the future.

For educational purposes, allow me to present to you this graphic presentation from the Federal Reserve Bank of St. Louis:

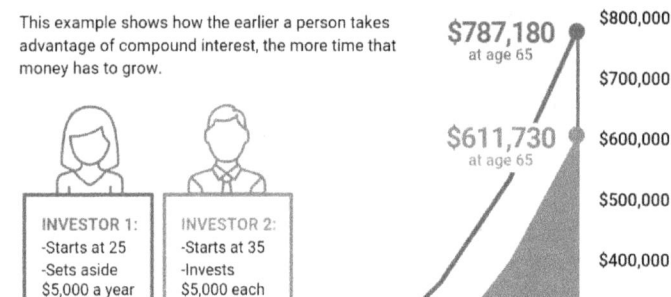

COMPOUND INTEREST:
WHO WILL EARN MORE?

This example shows how the earlier a person takes advantage of compound interest, the more time that money has to grow.

$787,180 at age 65

$611,730 at age 65

INVESTOR 1:
-Starts at 25
-Sets aside $5,000 a year for 10 years in a row.
-No more investments after age 34.

INVESTOR 2:
-Starts at 35
-Invests $5,000 each year for 30 years in a row until reaching age 65.

$800,000
$700,000
$600,000
$500,000
$400,000
$300,000
$200,000
$100,000

25 30 35 40 45 50 55 60 65

NOTES: Assumes an 8 percent interest rate, compounded annually. Balances shown are approximate.
SOURCE: Author's calculations.

FEDERAL RESERVE BANK of ST. LOUIS

In principle, one does not need a large salary or high income to end up with a million dollars or more, nor does one need to invest a large amount of money initially. The only requirement is to invest early, not at a later time. That is the secret to making yourself a millionaire: Time.

Chapter 9

KNOW YOUR
NET WORTH

"Make it a policy to know your net worth to the penny."

T. HARV EKER

The first step to being a millionaire is to account for what you have, what items you need (to spend money to acquire), and how much you make in a month or year. Don't just think about it; write these figures down. Traveling down the road to a million dollars is similar to hiking on a trail. First, you need a plan, strategies, and an organizational system. Next, you need to know how many supplies you can carry.

My daughter loves to hike and often goes out of state to get into the great outdoors. I've noticed that she continuously checks her provisions and backpack before leaving the house. She figures out what consumables she needs, assesses whether any item takes up too much space, and discards any excess.

The hike to reach your destination will be daunting and include many leaps and bounds. That is certainly true even in pursuing that first $10,000, $100,000, or the first million dollars. This goal may appear illusory, but it's not; it is achievable and doable. Whether your annual income is $45,000, $55,000, or $300,000, it is essential to know your net worth by heart before you embark on your financial journey. Know the items you spend on and what's left in your budget. Regarding your finances, you are the driver, hiker, assessor, and auditor, all bundled into one.

TURN YOUR EXPENSES INTO INCOME

Can you increase your income without really earning more? The key is to cut and trim your excesses. When you cut your expenses, the money you once used to pay for things you no longer need is transformed into income. You can invest in mutual funds or stocks or contribute to your tax-deferred account with the money you save. For example, if you stop buying a new $25 shirt or pair of pants every month and start bringing a packed lunch to work to avoid spending that $100 on food, you can save $125 monthly.

When we started in New York, my wife was the only one making the dough. I wanted to work, but I cared for the kids (a good alibi). Even then, we talked about money. When the kids were quiet in the evening, Leila and I would sit at the table and discuss our financial situation. We noted that the money that my wife was earning was slipping away just as fast as we paid for our routine expenses. Our apartment rental payment of $910 took the largest slice of the family income. Our savings were limping along and going nowhere.

A woman may earn more than a man—that's fine. But for me, a household with a woman as the breadwinner, while the man is content to just chauffeur his wife to work, is not an acceptable luxury. So we needed to do something.

Since our household income was then wholly dependent on my wife's salary, we realized we needed to cut our expenses to get ahead financially. We knew I needed to bring bread for the family table. That was the traditional and linear solution. It meant following these steps:

→ I needed to find a job or work to contribute to our household.

→ I needed to save and cut our expenses.

That was the two-step approach we were thinking of. There was just one problem. I wanted to work, but I was watching our kids (frankly, I had no "papers"). So I could not add to our income.

After much deliberation, we cut our expenses. We shared or rented out one of our rooms for $500 to a staff nurse who worked at the nearby Lincoln Hospital. And with the $500 we saved, we invested it in stocks mutual funds. The $500 we kept in the first month became $1000 in the second month. On the 11th month, we contributed $5,500. And that was only the beginning. When you cannot raise your income, cut your expenses. Remember: any expense you cut becomes income.

ASSET, LIABILITIES, AND NET WORTH

Knowing the specifics of your money is the backbone of good money management. It is essential to know the precise figures of your income, routine expenses, short-term debts, long-term debt liabilities, and any remaining balance to prevent financial surprises. Your net worth is the lean meat of your financial muscle. After deducting all your expenses and liabilities (or debts), it is a total net asset. Liabilities are the opposite. Liabilities are what you owe to others and your expenses: payment for water, gas, cable, rent or mortgage, and so on. It also includes expenses you do not ordinarily incur. Therefore, liability is negative as it does not add money or value.

WRITE THEM DOWN: YOUR ASSETS AND LIABILITIES

It would help if you regularly assess your assets and liabilities. Sit down with a pen and paper and calculate each figure for the last three or four months. Ask yourself, is the weight of your debt getting lighter or heavier?

→ Look at your record of expenses. Are there items on your credit card statement(s) that could have been avoided or shouldn't be there in the first place? Are there household expenses such as phone, cable, gas, electricity, water, dining out, clothing, and recreation that should be trimmed down or cut? Is your asset gaining more meat, or is your credit card gaining more weight?

When you know your income, assets, liabilities, or expenses including your net worth, you will have a better understanding of your financial health. You can make a good budget, plan your big-ticketed items, and make enlightened financial decisions. For example, if you know your regular expenses, and you have set aside an emergency fund, you can decide if you still need to add more money to your checking account for easier access, or if should you just put it toward long-term investments.

If you know your financial condition and possible expenses ahead of time, you can decide whether or not your whole family can travel out of the country to exotic places or just drive a mile away to the Chinese noodle house because that is what you can afford.

SUGGESTED CHECKLIST OF ITEMS TO KEEP TRACK OF YOUR FINANCES: (ARE THERE ITEMS OF EXPENDITURES THAT COULD HAVE BEEN AVOIDED OR ELIMINATED)

→ Get a notebook or record book to use as the annual record of your family finances.

→ Write down your weekly, biweekly, or monthly income.

→ Write down all your revolving expenses like car and life insurance premiums, electricity, internet, mobility, water, gas bills, etc.

→ Write down what you owe toward your mortgage, student loan balance, credit card balance, car loan balance, etc.

→ Write down the value of all your assets like a bank account, vested retirement or 401(k), 403(b) accounts, car value, house equity, etc.

→ Deduct your total liabilities from total assets. The result is your net worth.

A positive net worth should inspire you to plan, organize, and work to increase it (and maybe even loosen your belt and end your self-imposed deprivation). A negative net worth—means you have more liabilities than assets.

Here is a sample list of assets, liabilities/expenses, and net assets. (Thanks to the Minnesota Council on Economic Education in partnership with Federal Reserve Bank of St. Louis, Net Worth, and Cash Flow Making Personal Decision, 2019, for this information.)

INCOME:

→ Income from other jobs $250/month

→ Interest on savings $60/quarter ($20/month)

→ Stock dividends $75/quarter ($25/month)

→ Wages .... $36,000/year ($3,000/month)[9]

→ Total income $3,295/month

MONTHLY EXPENSES /LIABILITIES:

→ Cable/internet $100/month

→ Car loan payment $400/month

→ Cell phone service $60/month

→ Doctor visits .... $60/month after insurance

---

9   After income and payroll taxes

- → Electric bills $60/month

- → Gasoline $75/month

- → Groceries $200/week ($800/month)

- → Health club membership $40/month

- → Insurance premiums $100/month

- → Mortgage payment $1,400/month

- → Property taxes $300/quarter ($100/month)

- → Streaming television services $20/month

- → Total liabilities $3,215/month

AS PARTS OF THE ASSETS

- → 50-inch TV $700

- → Car value $9,000

- → Certificate of deposit $2,000

- → Emergency cash $600

- → Gold coins $2,500

- → House value $200,000

- → Motor scooter value............... $500

- → Savings $4,000

- → Stocks owned $10,000

- → Total assets $229,300

ALSO, ADD THESE TO YOUR ASSETS:

- → Your vested amount in 401(k), 403(b), or 457(b)

- → Cash value of your insurance

OTHER LIABILITIES:

- → Car loan balance $5,000

- → Credit card balance $1,600

- → Emergency credit card balance $500

- → Mortgage balance $150,000

- → Unpaid IOU $1,000

- → Total Net Worth $158,100

POSITIVE AND NEGATIVE NET WORTH

A negative net worth must be a wake-up call. No, it does not mean you are quick to spend your money. A negative net worth does not suggest you need reconstructive hand surgery for poorly handling your money. It is simply time to reconstruct your financial affairs. It means making a budget and looking at your household earnings and expenses. It also means tightening your belt, paying your debts, or putting money in tax-sheltered accounts. Above all, it means reframing your mindset to tame your financial behavior and lifestyle to improve your financial status.

On the other hand, a positive net worth means your assets are greater than the sum of your debts. It means that you still have assets after deducting all of your debts. This situation should inspire you even more, to continue improving your finances and keep on going. You deserve a pat on the back if you've achieved a positive net worth. Congratulations!

Chapter 10

THE RAINY DAYS FUND

"When it rains, it pours—figuratively and literally."

JOHN CORNYN

Intelligent financial planning must include setting aside funds for rainy days. By rainy day, I mean the time you have unexpected expenses or lose your source of income. So you need to prepare a fund to cover these situations. Your rainy-day fund is money for services or items not part of your ordinary or routine expenses.

Misfortunes can happen, and frequently, another one follows shortly after. One summer day, your car transmission fails while you are driving to work. Then, when you arrive home, your daughter tells you the home AC hasn't been working all day. Meanwhile, you hear your spouse in the laundry room complaining that the washer is acting like a dryer. That's when you start to feel the heat. Your body temperature starts to go up, and so does your stress level. You begin to ask silly questions that irritate everyone in the house. And if the situation wasn't bad enough, there is no money to spend on these unexpected expenses.

Having a fund readily available buys you peace of mind. It buys you a chance to regain your equilibrium. When a setback occurs, you just say, "No problem. We can call someone to come fix it." You may even say, "Let us replace everything that no longer works in this house." Your head is cool, and your stress level is down. Yes, when it rains, it pours—but that doesn't mean you have to get wet.

When my siblings and I grew up in the Philippines, our parents told us to save money for rainy days. As a kid, I had no idea why we needed to save for rainy days. I do not remember if we ever asked my parents why we should save for rainy days instead of sunny ones. Of course, that was a long time ago.

Saving for emergency expenses is the backbone of efficient financial management and good planning. Unfortunately, statistical studies have revealed that more and more working adults have no money or funds for emergency expenses. Why do they have no money for rainy days? Did they spend all their savings on sunny days? Either they are not heeding good financial advice, or they are simply boneheads. Keep the adage in mind: When it rains, it pours—and when it pours, a flood of misfortune could come your way. Do you have what you need to weather the storm?

EARNING $150K WITH NO MONEY FOR CAR TIRES

The pandemic that started sometime in 2020 resulted not only in a loss of lives but also brought untold economic destruction. With high inflation affecting this nation and the Covid 19 virus still hovering until early 2023, US household finances have not seen any improvement or recovery since the pandemic.

Even then, based on the US Financial Health Pulse survey, the AARP Public Policy Institute cited in its report written by Catherine S. Harvey in October 2019 that "53 percent of US households have no emergency savings account. The emergency savings challenge is widespread, including 51 percent of people over 50 and people at every income level." [10]Household income alone does not determine whether someone has an emergency savings account; structural factors, such as public policies that limit asset accumulation and individual behaviors, also play a role. Harvey added, "Americans at all income levels have no emergency savings account. Not surprisingly, the likelihood of having an emergency savings account increases with income. Nevertheless, significant shares of middle- and high-income Americans have no emergency savings account, while some low-income households do save. For example, one in four Americans earning over $150,000 has no emergency savings account."

This report by the AARP Public Policy Institute is confirmed by an earlier survey of Bankrate's Financial Security Index in January 2019, which shows a similar result: that only 40% of Americans could pay an unexpected $1,000 expense, such as a car repair or emergency room visit, from savings.[11] Based on those findings, Adrian D. Garcia further reported that "more than a third would need to borrow the money somehow—either with a credit card, a personal loan, or from family or friends. Another 14 percent would reduce spending on other things, while 10 percent would either figure out 'something else' or don't know what they would do."[12]

---

10   Harvey, "Unlocking the Potential of Emergency Savings Accounts."

11   Bankrate, "Financial Security Index."

12   Garcia, "Survey: Most Americans Wouldn't Cover a $1K Emergency with Savings."

This AARP Public Policy Institute report is alarming. It also reflects my observation: many nurses and healthcare workers lack money for rainy days. Why? I do not know. But I know this: if they want to put their houses in order, they must start to save for an emergency fund.

Remember, any sound fiscal management plan includes a budget for rainy days or emergency expenses. Financial discipline must consist of setting aside money for these situations to prevent disruptions in our pursuit of financial security when misfortune occurs.

WHEN ONE BAD THING HAPPENS, ANOTHER THING CAN GO BAD

When it rains, it pours. Sometimes, one misfortune is followed by another. It is nerve-racking when one bad thing happens after another, and we have no money to put everything back in order. We know that misfortune will strike, butweareneversurewhen. That'swhywemustplanandbudget for rainy days. Not only are we financially equipped for whatever comes our way, but we also maintain our sanity to handle the unexpected without detriment to our psychological equilibrium.

MANDATORY RESERVE

My nursing experience in an emergency room has given me valuable insight into what an emergency is — unexpected. This has given me practical insight into financial matters. When it comes to finances, I realized that there are uncertainties in life that exact unforeseen expenses. There is a need to set aside money for these unexpected expenses. We must have an emergency fund. I chose to call our emergency fund the Mandatory Reserve. It has $5,500 (Of course, setting aside more than $5,500 is even better). You can start your fund and give it a name. Call it Sugar Money or Sweet Honey Money—whatever you want, as long as your spouse knows to whom you are referring the name. Whatever name you call it, the purpose is the same: it is meant for emergency expenses.

Having an emergency fund can give us peace of mind. With $5,500 in the bank, you can afford a copay for an ER or doctor's visit. With that amount, you can replace your cracked windshields, buy new brake pads, or get new tires to keep your driving safe. With $5,500, you can replace your broken refrigerator or call an AC technician without hesitation on a hot summer day. You can do a lot of things with $5,500.

UMBRELLA FOR A RAINY DAY

The common advice that you must set aside a bigger emergency fund had me questioning — if one could hardly chip out money for a rain hat, how can you buy a bigger umbrella for a rainy day? Don't sweat it out. Start small and build your fund gradually. If you have a considerable sum of money stashed in long-term accounts, like 401k or mutual funds, and you and your spouse have stable jobs, a few thousand dollars allocated for long-term emergency expenses are good enough. Keep the extra money invested in long-term investments. After all, you can even make a hardship withdrawal from your retirement account when something bad turns to worse or borrow from it, and your payment goes back to your account.

Think about it. A few thousand dollars in an emergency fund is small. Still, the benefits of not having your life disrupted every time an emergency happens are not small. The emergency fund you set aside is part of a sound financial plan. Most importantly, it prevents you from breaking down emotionally or resorting to emergency borrowing at high-interest rates.

Now, let it work for you. Promise yourself that every month, maybe $50, $100, or more, will be set aside for the emergency fund. The amount is up to you— but start today or tomorrow, not next week. Open a savings account in your neighborhood bank or credit union solely for an emergency fund. A higher deposit is always better; a $50 monthly deposit is better than nothing. A $100 monthly deposit will become $1,000 in 10 months, while $125 set aside monthly will be $1,500 in 12 months. Your emergency fund will buy you peace of mind.

SAVE AT LEAST THREE MONTHS OF EXPENSES FOR LONGER RAINY DAYS

Sometimes, rainy days last longer than usual. Financial experts recommend saving for at least 3 to 6 months for long rainy days. Some experts recommend saving for 6 to 12 months if you become disabled or lose your job.

As a worker in the healthcare sector, you know that if you abruptly stopped working at your current position, you could always find another job in healthcare within one or two months with the same benefits. In addition, even during the recent recession, health facilities were hiring. With this in mind, consider how long you need to save and calculate your household essential expenses to determine how much you need. For instance, if your total household budget, including insurance premiums, amounts to $4,000 per month, then aim to save three to six times that amount or $12,000 for three months or $24,000 for six months reserve.

During hard times, cutting unnecessary expenses like subscriptions to online apps, magazines, club membership, cable TV, internet, or some phone lines that can be tossed aside is alright. But do not set aside or cancel any source of contingency. When worst comes to worst, do not give up your insurance policy, even if it has a cash value. You can always borrow from a cash value, but never surrender a policy with a cash value until you find new insurance and after the new insurance policy is effective. Remember: when it rains, it pours.

Chapter 11

RULE 72

"Many folks think they aren't good at earning money
when what they don't know is how to use it."

FRANK CLARK

Healthcare workers are hard workers. Many are hard-working, while only a few are hardly working. Seriously, most health workers work longer hours than they should. I saw doctors, lab scientists, registered nurses, housekeepers, or certified nursing assistants, they put in more working hours and hop from one job to another. Almost everyone is in hot pursuit of money regardless of wages or pay.

Letting your money work for you is vital, especially if you start early and take advantage of time and the power of compounding growth. The gap between what you have today and what you want to have tomorrow is not determined by your hourly pay, daily income, or salary; it is determined by what you do with your money and how wisely you make it work for you.

The problem with healthcare workers today is not their earning potential or ability to earn; it is the need for more basic knowledge about the factors that affect their money. How do we determine how long it will take for our money to achieve the desired growth? What interest rate do we need to pursue to double our investment? Here comes Rule 72!

ROLE OF RULE 72

Many in the healthcare setting have not heard of Rule 72. If you're among them, it's all right. No, it is not a law or a regulation crafted and passed by 72 members of the Senate. It is a mathematical formula to calculate when a particular amount invested at a specific rate will double by dividing 72 by that interest rate. This mathematical formula has practical applications for our everyday financial decisions. For example, we can use it to calculate when our unpaid credit card loan will double. Given a consistent birth rate, we can even use it to roughly estimate the population growth in our area.

According to financial experts Chris Thompson, a certified financial educator and planner finance (CEPF) of SmartAsset (Sept. 27, 2018), Rule 72 was known back in ancient times in Mesopotamian, Roman, and Greek civilizations. It is the fastest way to know how long your investment will take to double at a specific interest rate. Thompson wrote that Rule 72 was first mentioned by an Italian mathematician, Luca Pacioli, in his book Summa de Arithmetica, Geometria, Proportioni et Proportionalita published in 1494.[13]

Here is the Rule 72 formula:

$$72 \div \text{the compound annual interest rate (as a decimal)} = \text{the number of years until your investment doubles}$$

EXAMPLES:
Interest Rate and Time It Takes To Double Your Money

→ 72 / 12%......................6 years

---

13   Thompson, "Rule of 72 Defined."

→ 72 / 11% ....6 years and about six months

→ 72 / 10% ....7 years and about two months

→ 72 / 9% ....8 years

→ 72 / 8% ....9 years

→ 72 / 7% .... 10 years and about three months

→ 72 / 6% ....12 years

Rule 72 is a financial tool you can use to determine how much annual interest rate you need to quickly jump-start your economic growth by doubling your money. This effective financial tool will guide us to target an interest rate or return concerning the time and risk we can be comfortable with. The higher the return we pursue or, the higher the interest rate we want for our investment, the higher the risk.

Here's the formula:

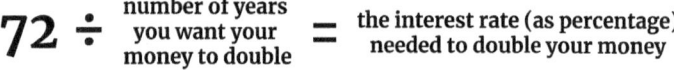

$$72 \div \text{number of years you want your money to double} = \text{the interest rate (as percentage) needed to double your money}$$

To determine the interest rate that will double your money in a specified amount of time, divide 72 by the number of years in which you want your money to double:

Years You Need to Double Your Money vs Interest You Need:

→ 72 / 5 years = 14.5%

→ 72 / 6 years = 12%

→ 72 / 7 years = 10%

→ 72 / 8 years = 9%

In the above illustration, if you want your money to double in six years, you will need a yearly interest rate of 12%. That is obtained by dividing 72 by 6, the number of years you want your money to double. The result is 12. So you need 12 percent.

For full transparency, I should mention here that financial experts claim that Rule 72 does not apply to interest rates lower than four. So no investor worth his salt will take a risk and wait a long time only to get a 3% interest rate.

To illustrate the concept of Rule 72: let us take the case of Calvin, a 35-year-old X-ray technician. Assuming he has $50,000 in a 401(k) invested in stock mutual funds paying a 9% compound annual interest, by the time he's 43, Calvin's original $50,000 will roughly double to $100,000 in 8 years without adding or contributing more. If that same $100,000 is continually invested in stock mutual funds for the same 9% compound annual rate of return, after another eight years, Calvin would have $200,000 when he reaches the age of 51.

Another example: Henry, a 45-year-old assistant physical therapist, and his 42-year-old wife, Bernadette, a licensed social worker, have a combined $475,000 in their

401(k) stock mutual fund, giving them an average annual compound rate of 7%. Using Rule 72, we estimate that in about 10 or 12 years, when Henry turns 56, and Bernadette is 54, the couple will have $950,000. And with the same 7% annual rate of return, Henry and Bernadette will have $1,700,000 at the age of 66 and 64 years old, respectively.

BANK INTEREST RATE

A colleague of mine, Nurse Gemma, and her husband, Nelson, a licensed practical nurse, are both 48 years old. They work extra shifts to save college funds for their two kids and deposit their money in the bank. They are conscientious workers. But they tend to be impatient because they are mostly overworked and don't get enough sleep. They would rather sleep than read about a 529b and other types of investments. They would instead pick up more extra shifts than educate themselves about basic personal finance topics such as tax-deferred accounts like Roth IRAs, 401(k)s, and other investment vehicles.

Nevertheless, they are proud depositors of their combined $350,000 income in the local Community Wealth Bank, where they earn 2%. Nurse Gemma told me this is the safest place for them to invest. She added that the bank teller offers the depositors a cup of coffee and cookies while waiting to be served.

Questions: Can we apply Rule 72 to determine the length of time the couple's money will have to work to attain double growth? Do Gemma and Nelson gain money on their combined deposit at a simple interest rate of 2%?

ANSWERS: No for both questions. The couple is losing the value of their money while it sits in the bank. Inflation at 3 to 5% minus taxes on their gains on deposit will erode their money's purchasing power. Assuming their money is "safely earning 2%" in the bank, it will probably take over 36 years to double the couple's original $350,000.

SUMMARY

Rule 72 is a valuable financial tool to determine the length of time for our money or investment to double, given a particular rate of return or interest rate. It can also give us important insight into the accompanying risk involved in a specific vehicle of investment that offers a higher rate of return. The higher the return on investment, the higher the risk.

Rule 72 can also guide people who want to take the risk to identify the vehicles of investment that offer a rate of return they can be comfortable with. Determining the return on investment, the risks, and the time to double the investment is an essential financial strategy.

Chapter 12

COMPOUND INTEREST VS. SIMPLE INTEREST

"Compounded interest is the most
powerful force in the universe."

ALBERT EINSTEIN

Let me start this chapter with a story. Mr. Jacobs is a wealthy owner of a large pharmaceutical company. One day, he called his trusted employees to his sickbed. Lawrence, a lawyer, was the first to arrive, followed by Dr. Healer, his physician. The third one was his nurse, Carlo, who had been with Mr. Jacobs for seven years. Carlo attends to the older man's personal needs. He ensures Mr. Jacobs gets to his medical appointments and takes medication on time. The last employee to arrive was Mr. Weissman, the accountant who had smartly guided the older man in his major business transactions.

From his sickbed, the wealthy man thanked his employees for their loyalty. As a reward for their services, he told his employees to select one out of these four choices:

→ Cash deposit of more than Three million dollars (Estimated $3,100,000)

→   A beautiful 3-bedroom farmhouse with an appraised
    value of $3,000,000 with some minor repairs needed.

→   Shares of stock of a pharmaceutical company worth
    about $3,200,000

→   A single favor they can only ask today with a value of
    not more than $3 million today. But the value may go
    up or down at a later time after the selection or after
    they receive the reward.

Mr. Jacobs reminded his employees that their rewards
are likely worth more when they receive them. The old man
told them they werefree to do anything after they received
the gift, including selling the farmhouse or the shares of
stock, but they needed to select.

The lawyer quickly stood, raised his hand, and declared,
"Sir, cash is king. I will take the Cashier's Check equivalent
to a cash deposit. Thank you." He smiled as he accepted
the check which is as good as cash.

The accountant chose the shares of the pharmaceutical company. He said, "Sir, I prefer to receive the company
shares. I don't mind waiting a few years to sell them for a
much higher value."

The doctor was hesitant, but eventually, he grabbed the
key to the farmhouse.

The old man looked at the nurse and asked what he
wanted. But the nurse said, "Sir, my state board of nursing
prohibits me from receiving anything of value from you. It
is unethical for me to accept a patient's money or property.
You are already paying me lavishly—that is enough for me."

The lawyer tapped the nurse's shoulder and said, "Young man, the law does not prohibit a nurse from accepting a gift out of a man's generosity." Nurse Carlo paused silently (while figuring out something he'd learned in his pharmacology class about compounded effects of medicines). Then, finally, Carlo told the old man, "Sir, I have no option left but to take number 4, and I have only a simple request. Give me just one cent, and double it every day for thirty-two days."

The lawyer commented, "Are you crazy, nurse? All you want from this wealthy man is just a penny?" The doctor ordered the nurse, "What you want is a peanut. Go and ask for more."

The accountant commented, " Let me calculate the balance after 32 days." A bit annoyed, the nurse maintained his decision to ask for only one cent, which doubles every day for 32 days. The old man quickly cut them, "Your request is granted, Mister Nurse. Thank you for taking care of me."

QUESTION: Who made the best choice? Can you figure it out?

THE ANSWER: It is because of the power of compound interest working in favor of Nurse Carlo.

I only appreciated the concept of compound interest when I saw its persuasive effects firsthand on the initial money we invested in stocks and mutual funds. After some time, we noticed that our seed money was generating money for us. Over time, our money is working for us. Believe me, compound interest is a magical force, especially when it's left to do its work in time.

COMPOUND INTEREST

Compound interest is an interest added to an interest earned on money deposited initially or borrowed. Wikipedia defines it as the addition of interest to the principal sum of a loan or deposit. According to a CNBC, featured on May 19, 2019, compound interest is the easiest way to double or even triple your investment or a surefire ticket to bankruptcy.

In this book, I have emphasized this subject to impress upon readers the exponential value of compounded return on investment. Hopefully, this information will prompt you to act soon rather than procrastinate.

THE POWER OF COMPOUND INTEREST

Compound interest can either make you rich or knock you down to bankruptcy. Compound interest is one of the reasons why there are people with a lower income but have a higher net worth than others who occupy higher positions or have higher earnings. The power of compounding growth exponentially turns small seed money into a fruit-bearing money tree.

On the other side of the coin, if you find yourself a borrower or debtor on compound interest, be prepared: compound interest is a tornado with exponential speed and the strength to cause severe financial devastation. If you get caught up in it, you will likely never be able to get out of debt. That is why the US Congress passed a law in 1968 called the Truth in Lending Act (TILA): to promote informed borrowers by requiring banks and financial companies to inform borrowers of the terms and conditions of the loan, such as the interest rate and whether it is a compound or a simple interest. You can find this TILA in the fine print accompanying your credit card, mortgage, or any other loan form.

TAKE NOTE: Do not throw out that piece of the paper that says, "Truth in Lending Act." It is the disclosure of the terms and conditions of your account. Please read it. Think three times if you can handle the loan you are signing and whether it imposes a compound interest.

UNDERSTAND THE FREQUENCY OF CALCULATION

An important thing to understand about compound interest is how often the interest is calculated, such as monthly or quarterly. This rate is called computing frequency. The more frequent the interest calculation, the faster the exponential growth of investment or money borrowed compared to every 12 months of calculating interest.

Imagine buying a newly minted $1,300 Apple iPhone 14 to replace your fully functional iPhone 8 on a credit card charging you 12% annual compound interest. (Believe me, I saw a lot of my coworkers doing just that.) Imagine having a household credit card balance of $12,000 and paying the minimum—on top of your college loan, car loan, mortgage, kids' tuition and allowance, and other obligations. Imagine your house AC breaking down beyond repair and needing a new $5,000 AC on store credit at annual compound interest to replace the old AC you bought with compound interest. Your problems are compounded.

In principle, compound interest on a debit or credit card is just as bad as being infected by a virus: it can compound your woes quickly. And borrowing money on a card with compound interest can be an even worse nightmare because it can bury you more profoundly in the sand. So watch out. Your best defense is to be mindful of the fine print before signing up or taking on new debts.

On the other hand, an investment that compounds over time is a sure ticket to wealth. So, as an investor, take advantage of the power of compounding interest (Please check the illustration in Chapter 8 by the St. Louis Federal Reserve Bank on the subject of compound interest).

SIMPLE INTEREST

Simple interest is money paid on the principal amount of money invested or borrowed. In the simple interest calculation, no interest is added to the original capital borrowed or invested to earn interest; interest is based only on the original money. Simple interest is typically what the bank offers you in your savings account.

To calculate simple interest, use this formula:

$I = P$ (principal) × R (interest rate) × T (time)

For practical purposes, let's study the benefits of both compound and simple interest in the overall management of our finances. Both compound and simple interest have profound effects on American households. Home ownership is made possible because simple interest is applied on mortgage loans when we buy a house. Imagine if your mortgage or home loan used compound interest. Who could ever afford to buy a house?

YOUR MORTGAGE

A mortgage is a guarantee to the lender that gave him the legal right to foreclose and sell the property made as collateral for the housing loan taken. Unlike most installment loans like credit cards, a mortgage loan is not a compound interest. You are fine if you pay the monthly mortgage on time or within the grace period. If you do not, after the due date or grace period, the mortgage company or the bank that lent you the money will demand payment and send you a late notice. After this, if you still do not pay, your lender will petition the court for foreclosure. The lender usually sets the due date for paying your mortgage on the first day of the month, but you have a 30-day grace period to pay your mortgage.

SHOULD YOU PAY YOUR MORTGAGE EARLY OR INVEST THAT EXTRA MONEY?

Many healthcare workers have mortgages or housing loans. A mortgage is a burden, especially for workers with other loans or debts. No wonder it is tempting to pay additional money to get rid of your mortgage. When you bring in extra money from pay raises, bonuses, tax refunds, or for working extra shifts, you might ask where the best place is to put that extra money. If you have a mortgage, you might wonder if you should send that extra money to your mortgage or invest it in mutual funds or your retirement account instead. Should you pay an additional $100 a month (or whatever amount) toward your mortgage so you can finish paying it off early, or should you invest that extra money?

Financial experts offer varying opinions, but here is what my wife and I did:

1. My wife and I maximized our contribution to our retirement accounts. Whatever extra money we had, we put in an emergency savings account, mutual funds, and a 529b college savings plan.

2. We did not put any extra money toward our mortgage.

Let me explain. My wife and I decided to maximize our contributions to our employer-sponsored tax-deferred accounts. Then, instead of paying that extra money to our lender, we put it toward our children's college fund and our mutual funds. We calculated that our money would grow more in the stock market or the tax-deferred accounts than the interest we were paying on our mortgage. I understand when people say that a fully paid house will give them peace of mind and a sense of security. But we ran the numbers, and the numbers did not lie. Sending the extra money to our retirement funds was simply more advantageous to us. A fat retirement account means more interesting places to see than being confined in a four-corner fully paid house.

YOU EARN YOUR MORTGAGE INTEREST RATE BY PAYING EXTRA

Our house loan was initially fixed at 3.75 % for 30 years. Paying extra money to the lender would be like earning the same rate as our mortgage—3.75 %—because the additional payment would be applied to our mortgage. Down the road, we refinanced our house to take advantage of a much lower interest rate (2.94%) for another 30 years. We put money from the house equity into a mutual fund. The mortgage interest is tax deductible.

Compare mortgage interest to the historical average annual return of the S&P 500 stock index from 1926 to 1918, which, according to Investopedia, is about 10 to 11%. Likewise, LPL Financial reports that for the past 90 years, the average annual return of the S&P 500 stock index is about 9.8%. So it's clear that by investing in stocks or mutual funds, our investment return is much higher than the 3.75% (or the 2.94% rate after we refinanced) on our mortgage. Homeowners merely earn the mortgage rate by paying extra. The money in our retirement account grows tax deferred. Our contributions to those retirement accounts and mortgage interest are tax deductible. Money in retirement accounts or mutual funds is liquid, meaning that you can access it on short notice, but a house is not. We don't mind carrying a mortgage for a few years at retirement until it is paid off; the interest is tax-deductible. It can offset some of our tax liability after retirement. The money we make from our combined retirement account balance and investments is more than enough for our mortgage payments.

As a practical matter, your creditors will love to see your house fully paid for. Still, they cannot touch your tax retirement money, including your 529b plan for your child's college education. (Check your state of residence.) So we have better options and more liquid assets than "house rich."

PAY YOUR MORTGAGE EARLY OR INVEST?

To discover the answer, let us look at the scholarly writings of the following financial experts:

In his article "Should I Pay Off My Mortgage," Hal M. Bundrick, a CFP and investment consultant, said that you are in an enviable position to pay your mortgage early if you have maximized your retirement account savings and set aside an emergency fund (usually three to six months). You still have a sizable amount of cash. He added, "A long-term fixed-rate mortgage is

an inflation hedge, with the risk of inflation assumed entirely by the lender. As the cost of living rises, your interest rate stays the same. Over time, the lender receives less valuable payments due to inflation. Rather than paying off your mortgage, investing the money may give you a higher return, especially in tax-advantaged or tax-free accounts."

Bundrick advocated prioritizing your retirement account, paying high-interest debts, and having an emergency fund. Likewise, homeowners can take advantage of inflation over time. For example, assuming a 2% inflation, your $1,000 monthly mortgage today is only $740 in 15 years.

In a Motley Fool article, "Pay Your Mortgage Early or Invest," well-known personal finance writer Christy Bieber wrote, "While owning your home free and clear seems attractive, it's important to consider whether paying off your mortgage early is a good financial decision. Paying a mortgage early will give you peace of mind and save you on interest."[14] However, according to Bieber, your house is not a liquid asset, so it is costly and difficult to extract money from it to meet financial needs.

She further noted that your assets are not diversified by putting more money into the house. "Sinking more of your money into your home means you'll be heavily invested in real estate. If your home declines in value, this will have an outsize impact on your net worth if you don't have money

---

14   Bieber, "Pay Your Mortgage Early or Invest?"

invested in other assets since extra cash went to bigger mortgage payments."

Bieber offered this example:

You have $300,000 on a 30-year fixed-rate mortgage at a 4.5% interest rate and pay $1,520 monthly. If you pay $1,820 monthly (with an extra $300 payment) instead of $1,520, you pay almost $80,000 less interest and pay off your loan in 21 years and six months. But, during that time, you've paid an extra $3,600 in mortgage payments each year. What if you instead invested $3,600 annually for 21 years, putting the money into an IRA or 401(k) and earning 7% on your investments? You'd have $161,514. That is more than double what you'd save in mortgage interest—so you'd end up with a higher total net worth even though you're still in debt. Ms. Bieber added, "Paying your mortgage early has big opportunity costs, and your net worth could be higher if you invest instead."

SUMMARY

Before paying extra money to your mortgage lender, use that extra money to pay yourself first to prepare for retirement. Increase your retirement contribution, pay down other debts, have an emergency fund, invest it in diversified mutual funds, or save that money for your child's college through a 529 b plan. Any amount of money left, then you can send it to your mortgage company. The extra mortgage payment of $100 or more can make a difference in cutting your mortgage term by four to six years. Rather than simply wanting to feel good about being mortgage-free, we must make a sound fiscal decision that positively impacts our overall financial security.

Chapter 13

FSA AND HSA: TAX FREE RIDE TO YOUR FUTURE

"The best things in life are tax-free."

COCO CHANEL

As a healthcare worker, one sure ticket to getting to millionaire status, even with an average income, is to follow the money-saving strategies being applied by those financially successful people. They will not succeed financially without financial tools or techniques they fully understand.

You have heard about the Roth IRA, the 403(b), the 457(b), and the other tax-deferred accounts that come with employment, but you may not know about the HSA and its little cousin, FSA. Both are equally important for sound financial planning and they can reduce the taxman's share of the pie. FSAs and HSAs are excellent financial strategies for saving money while deferring taxes. In addition, your contribution is tax-deductible, which can lower your taxes.

But here is the real kicker: unlike your IRA, 401(k), 403(b), and 457(b), the money you withdraw from your FSA and HSA for qualified expenses is also tax-free. Yes, that's right: tax-free. But before you get too excited, let us examine these accounts further.

FSA

FSA stands for Flexible Saving Account. It is like a savings account where you set aside tax-deductible money. In addition, the money may earn a little bit of tax-free interest in one year. And when you withdraw the money, it is also tax-free, provided that you spend it for out-of-pocket medical, vision, and dental expenses not covered by your health insurance.

FSA allows you to reduce your taxable income. Example: your annual salary is $70,000. You contributed a maximum of $3,050 to FSA. As a result, your taxable income will be reduced to $66,950. FSA is the best financial planning tool if you want to spend for some ophthalmic or optometric tests or procedures, eyeglasses, and other related expenses not fully covered by your vision insurance. You can also use it for non-emergency dental procedures such as new dentures, bridges, and implants, which are not fully covered by your dental insurance. It can tremendously save you money. Take note of this: for a simple cleaning, dental clinics will ask you to pay an additional amount on top of what they can charge your insurance. Your FSA money is perfect for these situations.

FSA Q&A

Let's look at the answers to a few commonly asked questions about FSAs so you can learn more about how this little-known savings strategy fits into your financial plans.

1. WHAT IS THE MAXIMUM AMOUNT YOU CAN CONTRIBUTE TO AN FSA?

The short answer is that anything is better than nothing. For 2023, the maximum amount you can set aside for an FSA is currently $3,050 in one year. If you are married, your spouse can also make a maximum contribution of $3,050 to FSA in the same year. The household total FSA contribution of $6,100 in one year can significantly reduce your taxes (when filing jointly). You can use the money to pay for any qualified vision, medical, or dental procedure, and related expenses for the family.

2. WHAT ARE QUALIFIED MEDICAL AND DENTAL EXPENSES?

The following categories of expenses qualify for payment with an FSA:

→ Prescription medications, including over-the-counter medicines with your doctor's prescription

→ Copayment and deductible expenses (meaning the amount you need to pay out of pocket before your insurance will kick in), except your health, vision, and dental insurance premiums

→ Medical devices or equipment such as crutches, wheelchairs, canes, respiratory devices, or blood sugar devices

→ Prescription glasses and sunglasses, contact lenses, and other eye care accessories and related items

→ Vitamins, First aid kits, skin care products, and feminine care may qualify. Gym membership, blood pressure monitor, and fees for weight programs are eligible expenses provided you obtain a Nurse Practitioner or doctor's letter of medical necessity or prescription.

3. WHO CAN AVAIL THEMSELVES OF THE BENEFITS OF AN FSA?

The employee who contributed to the fund, their spouse, and their dependents.

4. WHEN SHOULD THE FSA FUNDS BE USED?

The only drawback of this account, an employee, their spouse, and their dependents have only until the end of the plan year to use the money in their FSA. That's why the FSA is a strategic planning tool for foreseeable or planned vision, dental, or medical expenses.

5. WHAT HAPPENS TO THE UNUSED MONEY IN AN FSA?

At the end of the plan year, any unused money in the FSA will be considered lost—as in lost. For this reason, you should be careful to fund your FSA only with an amount sufficient to cover your family's planned medical, dental, and vision expenses.

REMEMBER: FSA money can be used for dental, vision, and medical expenses within the plan year.

6. IS THERE A GRACE PERIOD FOR SPENDING THE MONEY IN AN FSA?

Depending on your company or employer, there may be a grace period or carryover:

→ Your employer may offer you an option to carry $610 over the following year.

→ Your employer may extend by additional 2 ½ months to use your FSA money.

Take note: Your employer cannot offer both options. It can allow you to carry over up to $610 or extend the eligibility period for another 2 ½ months. Suppose you choose the carryover period but do not use the FSA money within that grace period. In that case, you will lose any unused portion of your money.

HSA

HSA, on the other hand, stands for Health Savings Account. The concept is similar to its little cousin, the FSA: pretax money can be set aside and saved in the account. But unlike an FSA, an HSA is wholly owned by the employee who opened the account.

The HSA has triple tax-free advantages:

→ The money you set aside in an HSA is tax deductible from your taxable income.

→ The money earns interest and grows tax-free.

→ That money is tax-free when you withdraw it for qualified medical, dental, and vision procedures or related expenses.

At this point, let me tell you: do not limit yourself to believing that the HSA is purely for medical, dental, and vision expenses. Far from it: there is an abundant list of eligible items you can spend your HSA money on. These items include everything from skin care products, weight loss programs, gym training, house filters, condoms, and special pillows to new beds—and that's just the tip of the iceberg. You can even use an HSA card to pay for your Amazon or Walmart purchases of the same or similar items that are health, medically related, or needed.

Take note: One basic requirement for setting up an HSA free from federal taxes is having a high-deductible health plan (HDHP). Based on the information at healthcare.gov, to open an HSA, the Internal Revenue Services or IRS treats a health insurance plan as a high-deductible health plan based on the minimum deductibles:

→ For 2023: A health insurance plan is an HDHP if the minimum yearly out-of-pocket expenses (total deductible) is $1,500 for individual coverage but not more than $7,500 for the same health network services. For a family, the total yearly deductible is at least $3,000 but not more than $15,000 for the same health network services.

Compared in 2022: The IRS considers a health insurance plan an HDHP if the yearly out-of-pocket expenses or total deductible is at least $1,400 for an individual and at least $2,800 for a family health plan, the same as for 2021. The only difference is the maximum limit of $7,050 for an individual and $14,100 for the family health plan for the same network services.

A health insurance plan is considered high deductible (an HDHP) when the policyholder or employee pays the initial cost of medical care before insurance kicks in and covers the rest. Compared to traditional health insurance, where the premium is higher but the deductible is lower (or there isn't one at all), with an HDHP, the premium is lower than traditional health insurance. Still, the policyholder pays a higher deductible before the insurance covers the rest of the vision, medical, or dental expenses.

With such a low threshold for a minimum yearly deduction, most health insurance plans employers offer today have deductibles that meet the IRS definition of an HDHP. Check your health plan for details.

Example of deductible: Nurse Mark has a $1000 deductible for covered medical services. He was brought to an emergency room. The cost: $1500. MRI cost $1000.00 and $500.00 for Surgery. Nurse Mark will pay the first $1000 for MRI as deductible and zero for surgical procedures. Meanwhile, another employee Andrew, a pharmacist, pays a $250 premium for an affordable health plan for himself, his wife, and his three children. But when he or any of his family members goes for a regular checkup, the deductible is $30, and the deductible for a prescription is $55. Let's say Andrew happens to visit the emergency room, and the deductible set by his health plan is $250. Andrew's ER visit costs a total of $500. He has to pay the initial $250 out of pocket before the insurance will cover the rest of the expenses. What if his emergency visit costs only $250? Andrew will pay for the entire cost of his ER visit. His insurance company will pay zero.

Suppose your family is young and healthy and does not engage in physically risky activities. In that case, an HSA offers an exponential growth advantage over other tax-deferred investments. Why? Because you will not be dipping into the HSA fund, especially when your HSA money is invested in a suitable vehicle of investments. High-deductible insurance with a lower premium is the obvious winner if the savings from the lower premium of your high-deductible insurance, plus any earnings or returns from the HSA investment, can approximate the minimum or equal the maximum deductible. That is because of the triple-tax-free advantage offered by HSA.

HSA Q&A

1. What are the advantages of an HSA?

HSAs offer triple tax advantages compared to any other tax-deferred accounts. In addition to these tax benefits, opening an HSA account at a younger age allows you to take advantage of compounding returns on your investment for years. The money can be withdrawn, tax-free, for any qualified dental, vision, or medical expenses when you retire early before Medicare kicks in at 65. Investing in an HSA is an excellent financial strategy if you plan to retire early.

Like any individual investment, you own the HSA account; it is not tied to your employer. You control which kind of investment you want to park your money in, and when you leave your job, you can maintain the same account.

HSAs offer a useful safety net. You and I have seen colleagues resign, retire, or take unplanned leave because their spouse or child became ill or needed medical care. Without an HSA, they might be forced to withdraw money from their 403(b), 401(k), or 457(b) accounts to cover specific medical bills, and these withdrawals always have tax consequences. With an HSA, the money is tax-free.

If, by God's grace, you and your spouse remain healthy at the age of 65, and you decide to withdraw money from your HSA to visit the famous Machu Picchu—or even try your luck in Las Vegas—you will pay only the ordinary income tax without incurring a penalty, just as with any retirement account.

2. How much can I contribute to my HSA?
For 2023, the IRS has prescribed a contribution limit of $3,850 for individuals, higher than the 2022 limit of $3,650.

For a family, the maximum contribution for 2023 is $7,750 compared to $7,300 in 2022. If you are 55 or older, you can make a catch-up contribution of an additional $1,000 for the year. Remember, the money can be rolled over year after year, and you can make annual contributions to your HSA based on the amount set each year by the IRS. Like your FSA, your contribution to HSA is tax deductible and 100% reduces your gross income. It grows tax-free, and you take your money tax-free for qualified expenses in the future.

3. Where can I open an HSA account?
Since you own the HSA account, you can check with any of your neighborhood banks, credit unions, and cooperative banks to see their offer. You can also open an account with Fidelity Investments, Vanguard Investments, T. Rowe Price, and other investment institutions, so check with these financial institutions.

SUMMARY

An HSA is a good investment strategy because it allows you to take advantage of these triple tax benefits:

→ Your contribution is tax-deductible.

→ The money in your HSA account grows tax-free.

→ You can withdraw money from your HSA account, which is tax-free if you use that money for medical, dental, or related expenses.

The only requirement to have an HSA is for you to have a high-deductible health plan (at least $1,500 for an individual or $3,000 for a family in 2023). Luckily, most employers offer HDHPs. Unlike an FSA, where you typically forfeit the unused portion of your money after a year, the money in an HSA is your own. Your account is unaffected by your employment change, and you can decide which financial institution will manage your money.

In short, an HSA is an excellent financial strategy if you intend to retire before age 65: you can withdraw the money tax-free to cover your medical bills and related expenses before Medicare kicks in at age 65. While it may not be very popular, an HSA is a powerful financial strategy in your overall financial planning.

Chapter 14

STOCKS AND DIVIDENDS

"Cash is trash."

RAY DALIO, BILLIONAIRE INVESTOR

Advancements in technology have ushered in revolutionary changes in the fields of medicine, mobility, gaming and connectivity, AI, robotics, and so many others. Likewise, changes in communications and aerospace have reduced the world into a small village of nations.

Anyone can profit from these phenomenal changes by investing in these companies. In addition, people with an entrepreneurial spirit can also benefit from these innovations.

Stock investment is one bedrock of building wealth. Countless Americans have become millionaires or even billionaires because of their stock investments in these companies. Just as the amino acid is the building block of life in the human body, stocks are the amino acid for building a solid cellular structure of wealth. Moreover, with time on the investor's side —they become the most potent multiplier for generating wealth.

You've probably heard of Warren Buffett, the living stock market investment legend. You may have also heard of Peter Lynch, another successful stock investor, and Benjamin Graham, who advocated for and is considered the father of value stock investing. We should give credit to these investment gurus for showing us the way.

But have you heard about a little-known woman who invested her small retirement money and turned it into multiple millions of dollars? Anne Scheiber, an IRS auditor who, in 1944, took early retirement with a small sum of money at age 51. Many articles were written about Anne Scheiber after she died in 1995 at 101 years old. She invested $5,000 in stocks when she retired. According to the article "How She Turned $5,000 into $22M" in Money magazine, Frank Lalli wrote that "in 1944, 10 years after Ms. Scheiber sustained a big loss in the stock market in 1933 and 1934 (through her younger brother Bernard), she started fresh with a $5,000 account at a firm of Merrill Lynch Pierce Fenner & Beane and slowly built her multimillion-dollar asset. By the time she died in January 1995, loveless and alone at 101, her assets were worth $22 million. As a tax auditor, she learned by poring over other people's tax returns that the surest way to get rich in America was to invest in stocks."[15]

Armed with this knowledge, she was encouraged to put her money in the stock market by buying good companies and reinvesting their dividends. In her will, Ms. Anne Scheiber left her money to Yeshiva University in New York and the Albert Einstein School of Medicine.

The words stock and stock market can sometimes have negative connotations; some consider the stock market speculative, risky, and akin to gambling. That explains why many people—including healthcare workers—shy away

---

15 Lalli, "How She Turned $5,000 into $22 Million (And How You Might Too...)."

from stock investments, saying, "Stocks are like gambling in a casino."

Let us talk about stocks. But first, let us start by discussing corporations. After all, without a corporation or company, there can be no stock.

WHAT IS A CORPORATION?

A corporation is an association or group of people who have united or organized themselves to engage in a business or commercial undertaking and have registered themselves as a corporation with the state by filing a document called the Articles of Incorporation. That complies with the legal requirements of the state authorizing the creation of a corporation.

A CORPORATION IS A PERSON

Once a corporation is duly registered with the state, it becomes a legal entity or a person with a personality. It acquires an existence different or separate from those comprising it -- incorporators, officers, managers, and stockholders. In the eyes of the law, a corporation is a person in itself (though this is only legal fiction).

A corporation is a legal creation; it has no actual or physical existence that you can touch or talk to; it only exists in the realm of the law. In reality, you only see the building or office and the people: the corporation's officers and staff.

As "a person," a corporation has some of the same rights as you and I. Like a natural person, a corporation can acquire assets, borrow money, and hold and sell properties. Like a natural person, a corporation can be sued and file a lawsuit to protect its reputation and interests. Corporations play significant roles in our lives. They can influence our thinking, change our lifestyle, and persuade us to adopt new products and tools daily.

BOARD OF DIRECTORS

The board of directors, in simple terms, is the group of people who run the corporation and make major decisions on its behalf, such as whether to acquire another corporation or property. The board of directors also decides whether or not to distribute the corporate profits to shareholders. It is a corporation's governing authority. These directors differ from the corporate president, chief executive officer, and other corporate officers involved in the company's day-to-day operations.

CERTIFICATE OF STOCKS

A corporation issues certificates of stock or shares of stock to the investors of the corporation, who are called shareholders or stockholders. These people either contributed money during the creation of a corporation or invested in it sometime during its operation. Corporations usually sell their stocks to investors when they need more capital to expand or acquire a business interest. Shares of stock represent equity or ownership in the corporation.

A corporation or company, in the course of its business operations, may need more funds or capital to pay down its debts or expand its business by buying other companies or properties. When a corporation decides to borrow money from the public, it issues bonds wherein it acknowledges its indebtedness to pay back the money borrowed, plus interest, to the creditors or holders of the bonds. (See Chapter 15 for information about bonds.) However, instead of borrowing money and paying interest, a corporation may raise more money or capital by issuing new shares of stock to sell to investors.

The stock exchange is the usual avenue for a company to sell shares to the general public or sell shares through a so-called private placement. In private placement, the company that wishes to raise money will negotiate with selected individual or institutional investors on the value of the equity investment of the company.

TERMINOLOGY

As initially mentioned, *stocks*, *shares* (of stock), and *equities* are used interchangeably to refer to ownership or equity issued by a corporation to its owners, officers, or investors. One share of stock represents a single unit of ownership in the company that issued that stock.

Dividends refer to a corporation's profit gained by engaging in business or from sales of corporate properties or assets acquired while doing business.

Dividends can be distributed in two ways:

→   The corporation can pay cash dividends, usually through checks sent to you or credited to your stockbroker account.

Instead of distributing cash dividends, the corporation can choose to declare or distribute stock dividends. This means investors will receive additional shares of stocks instead of money.

The corporation's board of directors decides whether to declare dividends in proportion to the stockholders' respective interests or the number of shares. These dividends can be distributed to stockholders quarterly, semiannually, or annually.

However, note that the corporation—acting through the board—can always decide not to declare a dividend, even if it has made an enormous profit. For example, the company may use surplus money to buy another company or expand its business.

EKG OF STOCKS

As health care professionals, we are familiar with the heart's electrical activities in various cardiac rhythms, as reflected in EKG tracing. Like an EKG graphic, stocks of a publicly traded corporation can display multiple rhythmic patterns. These patterns depend on many factors due to the stock market dynamics. For example, corporations are affected by the economic environment, and buyers and sellers all have different opinions about the value of a corporation's stocks.

One factor that affects the price of a stock is the general appreciation by the investors of the internal and external environment of the company. The external environment may refer to the laws, competing products and services, geographical locations, and new developments in the market.

Investors will be asking themselves: How good is corporate management? How stable are the products? Is the corporation able to handle the competition?

Investors look at the future of the company. They look at the potential of the company. As an investor, you are looking at the company's future based on how you assess its business today concerning its future profit, growth, market competition, and other factors. You buy stocks because you want your investment to grow. Not only that, but you also want to share in the company's profits. If you were to buy stock in a company today for $10 a share, you want to see your stock's value grow to $15, $20, or even $100 per share in the future.

Let us go back to the not-so-distant past. Before, people used a Rolodex (let's say it cost $75), a camera ($100), a voice recorder ($50), an alarm clock ($50), a GPS device ($150), a landline phone ($100), a small FM radio ($50), portable TV ($250), and a wrist watch ($100). It costs you nearly $1,000 to get out of bed and go about the day using all those gadgets. But, then, here comes Steve Jobs holding an Apple. Mr. Jobs crushed many companies and devalued the prices of many products by rolling out a revolutionary fruit of creativity—famously named the Apple iPhone—that put all these gadgets into one. Imagine if you had risked taking four or more bites of the Apple pie before it was ripe.

J.B. Maverick of Investopedia wrote in 2019 (4/14/2019), "If you have $100 and you bought just four shares of Apple (AAPL) at 23.30 on January 2, 2002, after some stock splits and phenomenal iPhone products, that original four shares became 56 shares."[16] Today, after multiple stock splits, the

---

16   Investopedia, "J.B. Maverick."

price of Apple is $161.82 per share. So if you purchased those four shares in 2002, your $100 would have become over $13,000. If you think your bank can offer such a windfall, think again.

But stock prices are only one indication of a corporation's health. A company that may be making good profits may not have the resources to sustain it in the future or maybe easily beaten by competitors with better products. Likewise, a company may have a good product or service today. Still, another company can always burst onto the scene and develop a superior service, technology, or device, perhaps one that increases speed, efficiency, or accuracy and revolutionizes communication, security, or disease treatment. Investors will chase after a company's stock that offers superior technology or products—even for a higher price—expecting to profit from the company's future income. A positive popular opinion about the company can also cause its stock to go up. That is the EKG of stocks.

Stock prices also fluctuate due to large-scale events like COVID-19, political conflict, the threat of war, and government policies. Events like these may bring stock prices down, which creates an opportunity for others to buy at a lower price. An investor with a long-term investment plan is like a critical care nurse, armed with knowledge about cardiac life support and Diltiazem (a calcium channel blocker), prepared to ride the arrhythmia of the stock market.

RIGHTS OR BENEFITS OF BEING A STOCKHOLDER

For educational purposes, let us briefly look at the rights of a company's stockholders. First, consider the case of

Doctor Fred, who owns shares in Microsoft. (Doctor Fred is an RN, but his colleagues love to call him Doctor Fred because he earns like a doctor and is always mistaken by patients as a doctor.)

EXAMPLE:

Doctor Fred purchased shares of Microsoft from his stockbroker back in 2017. He now owns a portion or fraction of the company in proportion to his number of shares. No one knows how many shares Doctor Fred owns. Still, he gives you the big smile of a satisfied man when you tell him he is a stockholder of one of the most admired companies in the world. He's especially proud because he bought his shares at a lower price and watched them appreciate.

As a stockholder, Doctor Fred has the following benefits and rights:

→ He can share in the company's profits in the form of dividends. If Doctor Fred has 5,000 shares of Microsoft, and the company issues a cash dividend of $2 per share, he can just multiply the dividend by his number of stocks to calculate his total dividend; he will get a total of $10,000 (5,000 × $2) —apart from any increase in value or price of the stocks. Sometimes, the company issues a stock dividend of two shares for every share or one for every share you hold. Cash dividends can be distributed to stockholders quarterly, semiannually, or annually. (Remember, just because a company made windfall profits does not always mean it will share those profits with its stockholders. The company may use that money to buy property, invest in another company or expand its business.)

→ He can participate in the election of the members of the board of directors (the governing body of a corporation) or appoint a proxy to represent him in the election.

→ He can inspect the corporation's books and records, including the incorporation articles.

→ He can attend the shareholder meetings the board of directors called for, ask questions, and share his opinions during company stockholder meetings.

Aside from receiving dividends, he can also earn another profit in the form of capital gains or an increase in the value of the shares. That is the most crucial benefit and advantage of investing in stocks. If Doctor Fred holds his stock investments for at least one year, depending on his filing status, and sells them, his tax rate will be between 0 and 15%.

CAPITAL GAINS

Capital gains refer to an increase in the investment's price or value when sold.

EXAMPLE:

Ms. Jamie Campbell, a physical therapist, bought 2,000 shares of NETFLIX (NFLX) at different times up until July 2009. She paid an average of $5.50 per share and spent $11,500. That was around 12 years ago when Netflix was just a DVD rental company. Fast forward to December 2021, Ms. Campbell decided to sell all 2,000 shares of Netflix at $374.59 per share.

This is how she made her money:

→ In 2009, Ms. Campbell's cost or capital was $11,100 for 2000 shares (plus assumed total brokerage fees of $100).

→ On December 2021, Ms. Campbell sold all 2,000 shares for $374.59 /share. Her total proceeds are $749,180—just in 12 years. Wow!

→ What is the capital gain per share? $369.09 for every share.

Take note: Do you know how much she will pay in taxes? If she is married and filing jointly with her spouse, the capital gains tax rate—that is, tax on her capital gains —would be a paltry 20%. By contrast, if this were ordinary income, the tax rate could be up as much as 37%.

The tax rate these rich people pay on the gain or profits (capital gains) from their stock investments is much lower than the rate your banks pay as interest on your deposit. But, hey, at least when you walk into your bank, you can stand on a red carpet while someone hands you cookies and tea.

HOW TO BUY STOCKS AND MUTUAL FUNDS

So how can you invest in stocks? The first step is to open a new account for this purpose, just as you would open an account in the bank. But this time, you're opening an account with a stock brokerage or investment bank licensed as a brokerage.

One way of investing in stocks is through mutual funds. A mutual fund is an investment where money from investors is pooled together to buy stocks or bonds managed by a team of investment experts. (See Chapter 15 for more on this type of investment vehicle.)

A stockbroker is a licensed agent who serves as the conduit between an investor who wants to buy or sell investment products like stocks and the market where stocks are traded (called, not surprisingly, the stock exchange). A stockbroker represents the investor in the stock market.

STOCK MARKET OR STOCK EXCHANGE

A stock exchange is a marketplace where companies are listed and shares are publicly traded through stock traders. Name a country: China, Nigeria, the United Kingdom, Germany, India, Mexico, or Brazil. They all have their stock exchange.

I highly recommend visiting the New York Stock Exchange on Wall Street in Manhattan. It is the world's biggest and most famous stock exchange, where billions of dollars worth of stocks are traded daily. That is why New York is the capital of the world.

STOCK INDICES

Think of your thumb as a specific stock index. Of course, you do thumb's up or down. The S&P 500, Russell, Dow

Jones, and Nasdaq are stock indices that show the stock market is up or down—you have seen and heard about these indices daily, five days a week. They are always part of the news cycle. You may have correctly associated these terms with the stock market but not aware of their correlation to your money.

Stock indices tell us whether the stock market in one sector or industry is up or down. For example, if the S&P is high, the market is generally high, while—for instance, the Dow Jones can be low (red), the Nasdaq can be high (blue), and the S&P can be red (down). Each index can independently point to an upward or downward projection. The upward or downward projection reflects a routine gyration of the stock prices in the market.

Like a tracing of an EKG, the market continuously fluctuates during the trading day. But you don't have to worry if you are invested for the long haul. When the indices are all high, people who invest in stocks are generally making money.

Let us look more closely at a few stock indices you're probably familiar with.

STANDARD AND POOR'S 500 (S&P 500)

The S&P 500 index is a basket of 500 companies representing the US economy. These companies represent various sectors of the economy, namely health care, oil and gas, transportation, banking and finance, industrial utilities, and computers. The most widely followed index, the S&P 500, fluctuates up and down during trading days. This index is one of the forecasting tools used to predict the direction of the US economy.

DOW JONES INDUSTRIAL AVERAGE (DOW 30)

Akhilesh Ganti, writing for Investopedia, explains that the Dow Jones Industrial Average, also known as the Dow 30, is a stock market index that tracks 30 large, publicly owned blue-chip companies being traded on the New York Stock Exchange and Nasdaq.[17] The Dow Jones is named after Charles Dow, who created the index in 1896 with his business partner Edward Jones. So when you hear on the radio that the Dow Jones is high or low, the broadcaster refers explicitly to the 30 companies tracked by the Dow 30.

NASDAQ COMPOSITE INDEX (NASDAQ)

In his Motley Fool newsletter article, "What Is the Nasdaq Composite Index?" Matthew Frankel, CFP, wrote that as of February 2020, 2,667 companies are included in the index. Only those companies exclusively listed in NASDAQ are included in the index. He added, "Nasdaq Composite is one of the most widely followed stock indexes in the US and is usually one of the three 'headline' indexes that market commentators often cite, along with the Dow Jones Industrial Average and the S&P 500."[18]

Like any other index, the Nasdaq fluctuates during trading hours. Because the Nasdaq has such a high concentration of companies in the technology sector—particularly of the younger, fast-growing variety—the Nasdaq Composite Index is often considered a good barometer of how well the tech market is performing.

---

17   Ganti and Scott, "Dow Jones Industrial Average (DJIA)."
18   Frankel, "What Is the Nasdaq Composite Index?"

Chapter 15

CORPORATE BONDS
AND MUNICIPAL BONDS

"Money is plentiful for those who understand
the laws which govern its acquisition."

GEORGE CLAYSON

Make no mistake: there are ways to make money without sweating it out. Investments don't have to be complicated; there are simpler forms of investments that healthcare workers can easily identify and invest their hard-earned money in, and with less risk than others. Of course, the less complicated it is, the easier it is to understand, and the more likely you will follow through. However, the returns on these investments are also lower than other riskier forms of investment.

In this chapter, you will learn about BONDS. In the simplest terms, investing in bonds is like lending money.

If a friend or neighbor asks to borrow money from you, you first size up the borrower: how can they pay you back? How is his business doing? Does he have other liabilities that can affect his ability to pay? What are his assets? Does he have other income sources to ensure you'll get your money back? These risk factors can and should impact your decisions to lend.

But when you invest in bonds, you lend money to the company, city, county, local government, or the country that issues the bonds. So when you invest in bonds, you could be lending money to your state—or even the great USA.

BONDS

A bond is a certificate or instrument of indebtedness issued by a borrower saying that it owes the lender or bond-holder money to be paid at a particular time—perhaps in 15, 25, or 30 years. The borrower periodically pays a fixed interest to the bondholder or bond investor until the appointed time when the bond is "called" or "matured," meaning the borrower has to pay back the face value of the bond. The debtor or borrower of these bonds could be a specific country like the United Kingdom, India, China, or Mexico. The borrower can be a city, state, county, or even your local school district or government agency. The borrower can also be a corporation or company.

Here are a few examples of entities you might lend your money to through bonds:

→ The City of Anaheim, California

→ LaGuardia Airport through the Port Authority of New York and New Jersey

→ The Los Angeles Unified School District

→ The Riverside University Health System of Riverside County, California

How does buying a bond differ from buying shares of stock in a company? With stocks, the stockholder owns a part of the company proportional to the number of shares owned. With bonds, the bondholder is a lender of money to the borrower but does not become an owner of that borrower.

MUNICIPAL BONDS

Municipal Bonds—often called Munis—are instruments of indebtedness or obligations from borrowers such as a State (of New York), cities, counties, and other local government entities. The borrower issues bonds to generate funds to build or repair public infrastructure and public utilities that benefit the people. For example, Nevada might issue bonds to generate funds to construct a temporary shelter for casino players too intoxicated to drive home. A county or government agency can also issue bonds. For example, Rockland County or the city of Portland might do so to raise money to build airports, expand public hospitals, repair local roads and bridges, or fund school buildings, animal shelters, and other essential services.

Investors of Munis are exempt from state and federal taxes.

So, for example, if Dr. Abraham has purchased bonds issued by the city of Portland, any interest that Dr. Abraham earns from those bonds are tax exempt not only from the federal government but also from the state of Oregon (because the city of Portland is the issuer of the bonds). Munis are also considered less risky than other forms of investment.

According to T. Rowe Price Investor magazine (Winter Edition, 2020), there are two types of munis:

→ General obligation bonds are money backed by the issuer's ability to raise funds through taxes. In bonds, if the state or city borrows money to fund a public program or build a public structure, it may pass an ordinance to levy additional taxes to pay the bonds.

→ Revenue bonds are bonds issued by government agencies or government-related entities to fund projects like hospitals or airports. The revenue these entities generate is used to pay interest and, ultimately, the principal debt to the investors.[19]

UNITED STATES TREASURY SHARES

Do you want to lend money to the United States of America? Wouldn't it feel great to be a lender when your borrower is the greatest country in the world? Well, you can! The United States of America borrows money by issuing bonds called US TREASURY BONDS, meaning that the US Department of the Treasury is the issuer of the bonds. Again, quoting from the US Securities and Exchange Commission at investor.gov, the bonds issued by the US Treasury on behalf of the Federal government "carry the full faith and credit of the US government, making them a safe and popular investment."[20]

Investor.gov notes that there are four types of US treasury shares:

19   T. Rowe Price, "Munis May Be Attractive for Fixed Income Investors."
20   U.S. Securities and Exchange Commission, "Municipal Bonds."

→ Treasury bills are short-term debts or securities that mature in a few days to 52 weeks.

→ Notes are longer-term securities that mature in 10 years.

→ Bonds are long-term securities that mature in 30 years and pay interest every six months.

Treasury Inflation-Protected Securities (TIPS) are bonds whose principal is adjusted based on changes in the Consumer Price Index (CPI is another measure of the average cost of consumer goods and services). TIPS pays interest every six months and matures in 5, 10, or 30 years.

CORPORATE BONDS

A corporate bond is a document or instrument of indebtedness issued by a private company or corporation as a borrower, acknowledging that the creditor will be paid interest plus principal upon the maturity date indicated in terms of the bond.

According to the US Securities and Exchange Commission at investor.gov, when companies want to expand operations or fund new business ventures, they often turn to the corporate bond market to borrow money.[21] A company determines how much it would like to borrow, then issues a bond offering in that amount. Investors who purchase those bonds are effectively lending their money to the company according to the terms established in the bond.

---

21   U.S. Securities and Exchange Commission, "Municipal Bonds."

Unlike equities or shares of stock, ownership of corporate bonds does not signify an ownership interest in the company that has issued the bonds. Instead, the company pays the investor a rate of interest over a period of time and repays the principal at the maturity date established back when the bond was issued.

While some corporate bonds have "redemption" or "call" features that can affect the maturity date, most will fall into the following two ranges of maturity:

→ Medium-term notes (with maturities ranging between 5 and 12 years)

→ Long-term bonds (with maturities greater than 12 years)

In addition to maturity, corporate bonds are also categorized by credit quality. Credit rating agencies such as Moody's Investors Service and Standard & Poor's provide independent analyses of corporate bond issuers, grading each issuer according to its creditworthiness. Corporate bond issuers with lower credit ratings tend to pay higher interest rates on their corporate bonds. Bondholders will receive periodic or regular interest payments.

BENEFITS OF INVESTING IN CORPORATE BONDS:

1. Safety. Bonds are generally safer than stocks. As a lender, your risk of loss is lower than it is in the stock market. In addition, bonds tend to hold their value, while stock prices can be volatile. (Note that corporate bonds are less safe than municipal bonds.)

2. Diversification. A Bond investment provides diversification among various bonds depending on the issuer. Corporate bonds differ from municipal bonds or US treasury shares issued by the government. Investing in corporate bonds spreads your risk from market loss from either government bonds or stocks. Corporate bonds also provide diversification in your investment in government bonds.

3. Higher income. Corporate bonds give higher income than bank deposits, municipal bonds, and stock dividends of companies. According to a leading investment company, PIMCO, in an article, "Corporate Bonds," corporate bonds have the potential to provide attractive income. Most corporate bonds pay on a fixed semiannual schedule. It added that corporate bonds yield higher than comparable maturity government bonds.

4. Liquidity. PIMCO reports that corporate bonds can be sold at any time before maturity in a large and active market.

COMMON OPTIONAL CORPORATE BOND FEATURES

Regardless of the type of bond, you should be aware of these alternative bond options.

Zero-coupon bonds do not pay interest; the bondholder will not receive regular interest payments. Zero-coupon bonds are issued or sold at a discount or lower than the face value of the bond. But, upon maturity, the bondholder will be paid at full face value.

Convertible bonds have the option of being converted into shares of company stock before they mature. Holders of convertible bonds usually exercise their right to convert those bonds into shares of stock of the issuing company.

INVESTMENT RISKS IN BONDS AND BOND CREDIT RATINGS

Yes, investing in bonds also carries risks like any other investment. Here are some of the common risk factors involved in buying bonds:

→ Rising Interest Rate. Bonds are generally sensitive to a rising interest rate. There is an inverse relationship between bonds and the interest rate set by the Federal Bank. When the interest rate goes up, the bond's price follows a downward projectile. Bond values tend to decrease when there is a reasonable expectation or perception that the interest rate will rise and increase when the interest rate is projected to decrease.

→ Default risk. Another risk factor is when the borrower company or the state, county, city, or government entity defaults or cannot repay the lender.

→ Bond credit rating. A downgraded rating of the company affects the valuation of the company's bonds. The company's ability to pay its debts is rated by Standard and Poor's and Moody's Investors Service (or Moody's for short).

Let's look deeper at the third factor, bond credit ratings, and how they can affect the investor's risk. A rating of AAA is the highest rating; a bond with this rating is known as investment grade. A lower grade AA and a single A grade follow the highly rated triple-A rate. The next lower grades are the BBB, BB, and B ratings. A bond rated C or D is risky; if the borrower is in bankruptcy proceedings, you are unlikely to recoup your investment. However, because of the risk involved, you can gain a higher yield when you invest in lower-rated bonds than in higher-rated ones. So, between a bond issued by a company rated as AAA and another rated as B, you may get better returns for taking a risk and investing in the bond graded lower. By rating the bonds, Standard and Poor's and Moody's provide some guidance to bond investors considering their bets and the ability of an issuer to pay its debts.

SUMMARY

When you invest in bonds, you become a lender to the company, city, state, government agency, or country that issued those bonds. As a bond investor or bondholder, you hold a debt security, not ownership or equity, in the borrower's property.

As a result, you receive a regular amount of money in interest as outlined in terms of the bond. In addition, the borrower or issuer of the bond will pay you, the bondholder, the full amount or face value of the bond at a specific future time called maturity.

In contrast, with stock investments, the owners of shares of stock have equity or ownership of the company in proportion to their number of shares. They receive their profit from the company in the form of dividends. When the company closes or goes bankrupt, the bondholders or creditors will be paid before the stockholders.

Chapter 16

MUTUAL FUNDS

"Don't put all your eggs in one basket."

MIGUEL DE CERVANTES

We are cautioned not to put all of our eggs in one basket. The advice contains practical wisdom. Nowadays, grocery bags are made of paper, and baskets are made of brittle materials. The bag can easily break—one considerable risk in an everyday experience like grocery shopping—and when you arrive home from the grocery store, you might be surprised that half a dozen eggs are broken. The trunk of your car is all slimy because the basket rolled over or fell inside the chest. See how risky it is to put your eggs in one basket? This adage also has practical applications in how we invest our money.

If you have $20,000 and deposit all of it in your bank savings account, the whole amount is like your eggs, and your bank account is like a single basket for all your eggs. The bank gives you 2.0 to 2.5% interest, added to your ordinary taxable income. But do you think your eggs are safe? No! In fact, inflation erodes the value of your nest eggs because your money does not grow enough in the bank to catch up with the increasing prices of goods and services. Your bank may give you up to 3.5% interest, but if inflation is roughly 7%, you are losing money in the long run. And that's not all: because you did not diversify or spread your money among different vehicles of investments, you have increased the risk to your nest eggs by failing to take advantage of compounding growth opportunities.

YOUR HOUSE CAN BE A BASKET OF EGGS

You have $15,000 cash and decide to put all of it towards your mortgage (with an interest rate of 3.0%) on top of your regular monthly mortgage payment. Your house can be considered a basket. Because you put that extra $15,000 toward your mortgage, you missed an opportunity to either diversify by investing that extra money in other investments or by putting some amount to increase your contribution to your 401(k) to gain a higher return. Your mortgage interest will remain at 3.0% and lower than what you would get by investing that money in stocks, mutual funds, 401(k), and similar accounts. Further, the value of your home could fall as it did during the 2008 recession.

Here's another example that illustrates the value of this adage: You have the same $15,000, and you decide to invest it all in stocks of a single company. Your basket here is the single company where you invested your money. If the company happens to go south due to poor management or competition, your stock will also lose value. Your stock concentration in one single company exposes your money to greater risk.

MUTUAL FUNDS

My first foray into stocks and bonds was through mutual funds. Many healthcare workers have a limited understanding of Mutual Funds, and those who have heard about them tend to misunderstand them. So allow me to acquaint you with this type of investment.

To simplify, mutual means something is held or shared by a group of people with common goals. A mutual fund is, therefore, a type of investment wherein monies invested by the people (the investors) are placed in a common fund with a common objective. The Fund is professionally managed by individuals or groups with professional expertise in finance, investment, and research.

The funds are invested in various bonds, company stocks, or a mix of stocks and bonds. Any gains or profits from those investments and losses are divided among the investors in proportion to their number of units or shares in the mutual fund. The price of the share or unit is referred to as its Net Asset Value (NAV).

According to the Fidelity Learning Center, "Mutual funds are investment strategies that allow you to pool your money together with other investors to purchase a collection of stocks, bonds, or other securities that might be difficult to recreate on your own. The collection of stocks where the funds are invested is referred to as a Portfolio."[22]

Further, according to the US Securities and Exchange Commission at investor.gov, "A mutual fund is a company that pools money from investors and invests the money in securities such as stocks, bonds, and short-term debt."[23] Investors buy shares in mutual funds, and each share represents an investor's portion of ownership in the fund and the income it generates.

---

22   Fidelity Learning Center, "What Are Mutual Funds?"
23   U.S. Securities and Exchange Commission, "Mutual Funds."

In mutual funds, there is Diversification, meaning you invest in the stocks of several companies across various industries and sizes in multiple countries. Professional money managers manage mutual funds with their own researchers and investment analysts. That is the meaning of not putting all your eggs in one basket; the risk to your investment is minimized because you own stock of several companies in the portfolio. If one company fails to meet investors' expectations and the company shares of stocks lose their value, the other companies in the portfolio help to offset the loss and increase the total value of the portfolio.

MUTUAL FUND BENEFITS

In summary, these are the four key benefits of mutual funds:

1. YOU CAN DIVERSIFY YOUR ASSETS

When you invest in a mutual fund, your money is pooled with other people's investments. The fund buys or invests in the shares of stock of several companies engaged in various businesses such as telecommunication, agriculture and environment, information technology, defense, banking, cybersecurity, medicine, and health care.

Through mutual funds, you can also invest in companies doing business in other parts of the world, such as a mining company involved in rare earth explorations in Kagmasusu, Somalia, or in the remote mountains of Timbuktu in the Philippines. In addition, by investing in mutual funds, you can invest your money in companies focused on or located in Nigeria, China, France, Japan, Italy, Singapore, or Canada. That explains why you hear international funds, world funds, global mutual funds, China funds, and Latin America funds.

Mutual funds allow you to invest in small, large, and medium-sized companies. You can also concentrate or focus your investments on a particular sector of the economy, such as financial, technology, consumer, or healthcare companies through mutual funds like Fidelity Small Cap Growth Fund, Vanguard Energy Fund, Fidelity Technology, or T. Rowe Price Financial Services Fund.

2. YOUR INVESTMENT RISK IS MINIMIZED
Suppose one, three, or five companies in the fund portfolio fail to meet the expectations of investors and lose their value. In that case, several other companies in the portfolio can compensate for those losses. Further, mutual funds are managed by experts. These investment professionals are experienced in market research and trained to identify companies with excellent prospects to invest in.

According to an Investopedia article on Diversification by Troy Segal, "Studies and mathematical models have shown that maintaining a well-diversified portfolio of 25 to 30 stocks yields the most cost-effective level of risk reduction. Diversification is a risk management strategy that mixes various investments within a portfolio."[24]

3. YOU CAN INVEST WITH LESS
As mentioned earlier, my first stock investment was with a mutual fund. With my minimum investment of $50 or $100 a month, I was able to participate in the profits of several companies through mutual funds — that I may not have

---

24   Segal, "Diversification."

personally been able to attain by investing in an individual company on my own.

Consider this: as of December 9, 2019, it cost $1,1749 to buy one single share of Amazon—but way back on November 9, 2001, the price per share was just $7.15, and on November 16, 2009, the price per share was $51.59. How many healthcare workers will ever find out about Amazon in its early stage?

In a word, you can start investing in Mutual Funds for as little as $100 or $500, but investing in an individual company's share of stocks will require you more. Likewise, by investing in Mutual Funds, you leverage the expertise of people experts in research and in identifying those Amazons — the disruptor of businesses at the earliest stage.

4. EXPERTS MANAGE YOUR INVESTMENT

When you invest in mutual funds, people with expertise in statistics, research, financial analysis, and economics are at your disposal. These professionals are part of the management of the company overseeing the day-to-day operations of the fund. They select and identify which companies to invest in, whether in the US or abroad, and whether they are small, medium, or large-size companies. As an investor, you can use leverage. Remember leverage?

EXPENSE RATIO

Open the Sunday newspaper and look at its business section. You will see various financial and investment companies like Fidelity, T. Rowe Price, and others with their long list of mutual funds. There are close to 1,000 mutual funds to choose from. One consideration when deciding which mutual fund to invest in is the expense ratio or annual percentage rate charged to you for the cost of investing, operating, and managing the fund. The expense ratio can be .05% or 1.0%, or 1.5%, and it can go as high as 2.5%; the lowest is .05% means it is the lowest expense ratio. That means a certain percentage of the total profit is deducted from what could have otherwise been your profit. The higher the expense ratio, the higher the cost, and the bigger the bite into your investment return over time.

Likewise, take note of so-called loads. The term load simply means the fees for investing or buying into a mutual fund. Front-end load means the fees or charges for investing in the fund. A back-end load means the fees or charges for selling your investment in the fund (but these fees are usually waived after you hold your fund for a year).

Take note: The best approach is to invest in mutual funds with a low expense ratio and no loads or fees. If you want to invest in stocks and bonds through mutual funds, you might consider the following:

- → Vanguard Funds

- → T. Rowe Price Funds

- → Fidelity Funds

- → Charles Schwab

- → American Century Funds

As a long-term investor, you need to work with a Certified Financial Planner (CFP) in your area who can tailor an investment plan specific to your situation and goals.

Chapter 17

401(K), 403(B), AND 457(B)

"A penny saved is worth two pennies earned after taxes."

RANDY THURMAN

The linchpin of financial security in retirement is the value of your nest egg in your 401(k), 403(b), or 457(b) accounts and other savings accounts.

It is a widespread belief that an ordinary worker whose income depends on employment will never succeed at becoming a millionaire. This belief has a debilitating effect on workers. The fact is, there are countless ordinary American workers— including the guy you called a pinhead behind his back— who have found the secret to decoding the seemingly secret formula contained in the IRS Code sections 401(k), 403(b), and 457(b). These IRS Code sections have proven to transform countless American workers into millionaires, one paycheck at a time. All they did was to automate their seed money to come out of their paycheck, then allow time to grow their money at a compounding rate of returns tax-free.

These IRS Code sections 401(k), 403(b), and 457(b) share the same genetic makeup: they are all tax-sheltered retirement accounts. Your contribution to the account is tax-deductible from your taxable income. The earnings or profits are not taxed until withdrawn at a certain age or at the time of retirement. The only significant difference among these three siblings —401(k), 403(b), and 457(b) — lies in what kind of employer offers the benefits. Private employers or for-profit companies offer 401(k) to their employees. The 457(b) is provided to employees of counties, cities, local governments, or its agencies. On the other hand, non-profit organizations and tax-exempt companies, including hospitals and schools, offer 403(b) to employees. Hospitals and various healthcare companies that sponsor 401(k) s or 403(b)s may also match the employee's contribution dollar for dollar up to 5% of the worker's gross earnings. This matching contribution from the employer is free money put on the table by the employers for their employees to grab through tax-sheltered accounts. It does not take rocket science to know that many ordinary workers who use this magic formula retire as millionaires.

Unfortunately, many employees, especially in health care, have procrastinated or are still asleep in the noodle house, ignorant of these tax-deferred accounts because they either do not know there are such things as tax-sheltered accounts or simply don't care to learn. That explains why such a high percentage of employees nearing retirement have ended up with dismally low savings (or none at all) in a 401(k), 403(b), or 457(b). If their primary source of retirement income is their Social Security benefits, they are in an ugly situation.

Before the 2020 Pandemic, American households had dismal savings. The Pandemic was followed by a high inflation rate in 2022 and 2023 which added a burden to Americans. Jeanette Settembre explains, "The average annual Social Security retirement benefit is $17,500 this year (2019), with a 1.6% cost-of-living increase slated for 2020. The National Institute of Retirement Security found that this uneven distribution of wealth, coupled with shockingly low retirement savings among most households, could be a threat to working Americans nearing retirement. Indeed, 59% of working Americans don't have retirement savings like 401(k)s or individual retirement accounts (IRAs). The wealth gap is making retired Americans financially vulnerable, research suggests."[25]

SHERREL'S STORY

Remember the story of Sherrel? She began working as a staff nursing assistant when she was only 23. She worked in a nursing home for 12 years without knowing that a 401(k) was available from her employer. She only heard about it later from her coworkers when she was leaving the company. Imagine: had Sherrel put at least 5% of her $50,000 gross income (including extra shifts) into her 401(k), that would have been $2,500 in a year. That is very affordable and doable. And assuming that her employer offered a matching dollar-for-dollar contribution of up to 5% of their employee's gross income, that would have been $2,500 up for grabs. She could have set aside $5,000 in a single year in her tax-sheltered account.

Now, let us assume Sherrel had contributed to her 401(k) for just ten years and then stopped at age 35. Her money would have grown to $787,000 at age 65, assuming an average 8% annual compounded return. That is based on just ten years of contribution and nothing more. Imagine if she was contributing to her employer's 401(k) that whole time.

Those ten years are gone now, and Sherrel can never return them. They say never to cry over spilled milk, but we

25   Settembre, "Retired Americans at Risk Financially as Wealth Gap Widens."

must learn to clean up after ourselves. Without a doubt, time is your best ally on your way to becoming a millionaire.

Here's a closer look:

→ The employee's gross income = $50,000/year

→ 5% of gross income contributed to 401(k) = $2,500/year

→ The employer's matching dollar-for-dollar contribution up to 5% of the employee's salary = $2,500/year

→ Total annual money going into the account = $5,000 × 10 years = $50,000

Suppose both employee and employer give a total of $5,000 yearly since the employee was only 23 and stop when the employee is 35, at a compounded return of 8% until 65 years old. In that case, the investment will grow to roughly $787,000 without any additional contribution from age 35 when Sherrel left that job.

Take note: For the year 2023, the maximum amount that an employee or worker can contribute to 401(k), 403(b), or 457(b) is $22,500. If you are age 50 and above, you can make a catch-up contribution of an additional $7,500 for a total of $30,000 in one year. The yearly contribution increases.

BERNARD AND MARGIE
Let's look at the case of Bernard Samaritan, a dialysis technician from Rockland County, New York. He is married to Margie, a unit clerk at the local hospital. Bernard earns about $70,000 annually, and his wife adds about $55,000

to their household income. The couple set aside 20% of their gross income to their 401(k)s for a combined total of $25,000 a year. The hospital matches 50 cents of every dollar of employee contribution up to 6% of their gross income, equivalent to $3,950. The couple has contributed to their 401(k) for 25 years. Today, the Samaritan couple has about $1,200,000. Every year, the Samaritan couple gets a small tax refund because their gross income is reduced by $25,000, the amount they set aside in their tax-sheltered accounts.

Bernard told me their current house is fully paid for. They sold their first house and applied the equity toward the second house. Bernard told me he loses sleep over debts and has been putting in extra shifts to speed up his debt payments.

Let's look at the numbers:

The couple's yearly gross = $125,000

20% of gross income contributed to 401(k)s = $25,000. The employer's 50% contribution up to 6% of the employee's contribution, roughly $3,950

Total yearly savings = $28,950

RETIREMENT ACCOUNTS Q&A

Let's look at the answers to some commonly asked questions about retirement accounts:

1. What is a vested account?

Vested means the employee or worker has acquired a proprietary right or ownership to the employer or company matching contribution to the employee retirement account after working for the employer for a certain period (usually five years). When you acquire a vested interest or right, you can roll over or transfer all the monies in the fund to your new employer-sponsored retirement account.

2. If I quit or leave my job, what will happen to the money in my 401(k), 403(b), or 457(b)?

When you leave your job for greener pastures or for whatever reason, you have a few options for handling your employer-sponsored retirement account:

→ Leave your fund with your old employer-sponsored retirement account. It will grow just the same at a compounded return. If you are vested in the account, the employer contribution is yours and becomes part of the fund. You can transfer the entire fund to another retirement account offered by your new employer.

→ Open an IRA account with the bank or financial institution of your choice and transfer the fund in your old 401(k), 403(b), or 457(b) account to that institution for management.

Take note: If you leave your job and take the money with you or deposit it in your personal bank account, or spend it, you will pay a penalty of 10% on top of the taxes on your withdrawal.

3. Can I withdraw money from my 401(k), 403(b), or 457(b)?

Yes, an employee can withdraw some or all of the money from their account in financial hardship, disability, job loss, sickness not fully covered by health insurance, or other unfortunate circumstances without penalty. You can also withdraw from these types of accounts to use the money to buy your first house or pay for children's college tuition and other related expenses. A hardship withdrawal is an "immediate and heavy financial need" for the fund to pay for medical bills, college tuition fees, costs for funerals, or withdrawal to avoid foreclosure or eviction.

4. Can I borrow from my tax-sheltered retirement account?

Yes, you can borrow from your 401(k), 403(b), or 457(b) accounts without regard to your credit profile or score. You pay a lower interest rate than the rate offered by your bank or credit cards; the money you paid in interest goes to your account. But take note: many financial experts discourage the practice of borrowing money from your retirement account because the money would grow more money for you if it remained invested.

5. Can a creditor collect on my 401(k) or other tax-sheltered account?

No, your creditor cannot collect or charge your 401(k), 403(b), or 457(b) funds. The Employee Retirement Income Security Act of 1974 protects your money in tax-sheltered accounts from your creditors' hands. How many people with substantial assets in retirement funds still file for bankruptcy and win in court over their creditors? No wonder you saw that pinhead with millions in his 457(b) or 401k accounts was laughing on his way out of court after facing his creditors before the judge.

SUMMARY:

These 401(k), 457(b), or 403(b)s are tax-sheltered accounts that allow employees to deduct pretax money automatically from their paychecks. That money can be invested in funds that buy stocks and/or bonds.

The employee's contribution, including the matching contribution from the employer, can grow tax-free on a compounded return until the employee withdraws the money from the fund in retirement, usually upon age 59.

By deducting the retirement contribution from the worker's gross income, the taxable income is lowered, and so is the tax bracket. This results in lower income taxes.

The main purpose of these accounts is to secure workers' financial well-being upon retirement. Ant withdrawal from the fund before age 59 ½—or before retirement, as in the case of a 457(b)—the corresponding penalty is 10%. The employee will pay taxes on the money withdrawn. An employee can borrow from the fund at a lower interest rate than other lenders. Still, money paid as interest is returned to the account.

Every year, the amount of money an employee can set aside in a tax-sheltered account increases. For 2023, an employee can contribute a maximum of $22,500 compared to 2022, which is $20,500. And if an employee is 50 years or older, he or she can contribute an additional $7,500 (called catch-up contribution) for $30,000 in 2023. Again, this can significantly reduce the taxable income of the employee.

If you plan to leave your employer, you should know when you become fully vested so that all the monies in your retirement account can be rolled over or transferred to the new employer. When you are vested, you can transfer your contribution and employer-matching contribution to the account.

It is a great irony that the IRS Code being used as a weapon by the most feared US taxmen to extend their long arms and extract tax money from all of us is the same IRS Code that hundreds of thousands of ordinary American workers used as armor to shield them from the same long arm. By decoding the IRS Code, ordinary workers can make themselves into millionaires—including that guy you called a pinhead. Once again, it is not what you earn that makes you financially secure in retirement. It is how much you set aside and how well you manage what you have set aside that matters.

Chapter 18

ROTH IRA & TRADITIONAL IRA

*The importance of money flows from it being a
link between the present and the future.*

JOHN MAYNARD KEYNES

What you will have in the future depends on where you invest your money and how early you begin. Even with a small monthly investment, your money will grow faster through the power of compounding return, especially in a tax-deferred investment vehicle.

Aside from your employer-sponsored retirement account, there are other tax-haven vehicles of investment where either your pretax or your after-tax money can ride for a compounded trip. When you have money in these accounts, your money grows without you having to pay any taxes. These are great investment vehicles for building and securing your future. With these financial tools, you can harness the power of compounding returns on your money. The Roth IRA and the traditional IRA (often called the IRA) are truly great options outside your employer-sponsored tax-deferred accounts for reaching a million dollars over time.

ROTH IRA

A Roth IRA is a kind of individual retirement account (IRA) identified with its leading proponent, Senator William Roth, from Delaware. According to Wikipedia, the Roth IRA is a modification of the original IRA sponsored by Senator Roth and Senator Bob Packwood. Originally called an IRA Plus, Oregon Senator Bob Packwood and Senator Roth in 1989 proposed the idea. The Packwood–Roth plan allows individuals to invest up to $2,000 in an account without immediate tax deductions. The earnings could later be withdrawn tax-free at retirement. Based on this plan, the Roth IRA was established by the Taxpayer Relief Act of 1997.

A Roth IRA, also known as a Roth, is a kind of individual retirement account where an individual can contribute after-tax money (the money you receive after paying taxes on it) to a fund. The money you contribute to this fund, plus any earnings such as dividends and capital gains, can grow on compounded returns tax-free. Then, you can withdraw money from the Roth, also tax-free, provided you meet the following requirements:

1) You are 59 ½ years old at the time of your withdrawal.

2) You have held the money in your Roth and maintained the account for at least five years.

Roth is an individual retirement account intended for retirement or as a safety net. But more than that, the double tax advantage of Roth makes it a powerful financial tool for ordinary Americans to build a fortune. A Roth account is also a powerful strategy to avoid future tax, including any impact from future tax increases, especially if you look forward to a higher income later or after retirement.

TAKE NOTE:

You can withdraw your Roth contribution without paying the penalty or taxes even before five years or before you reach 59 ½-year-old. Anyway, it's your money already taxed before you place it into the Roth account. You can leave any earnings in the account growing at compounded return without taxes until you withdraw it tax-free and without penalty, provided you satisfy the requirements.

If you withdraw the earnings of your money contributed to Roth before you are 59 ½ years old or without waiting five years to hold your account, the penalty is 10%. You will also pay taxes on your withdrawal.

ROTH IRA Q&A

Let's look at the answers to a few common questions about Roth IRAs.

1. Can I withdraw my money from a Roth without a penalty?

Yes, in some cases. Just like with employer-sponsored retirement accounts such as 401(k), 457(b), or 403(b), you can withdraw money from your Roth IRA without a penalty for these reasons:

→ You are a first-time home buyer

→ You are permanently disabled

→ For qualified educational expenses

→   You withdraw the Roth money for medical expenses not covered by your health insurance.

Upon your death, your account beneficiary can withdraw the money without penalty.

2. How much can I contribute to a Roth IRA?
For 2023, you can contribute a maximum of $6,500. Again, if you are 50 years old or over, you can make an additional catch-up contribution of $1,000, a total of $7,500 for a year.

a) If you are single, head of household, or married filing separately, you can make a total contribution, provided that your modified adjusted gross income is less than $138,000; otherwise, your contribution is reduced if you make more than $138,000. If your income is $153,000 or over, no contribution is allowed.

b) However, if you are married, and filing jointly, or a qualifying widower, your modified adjusted gross income must be less than $218,000 to be able to put in a maximum contribution to ROTH IRA; otherwise, you can make only a partial or reduced contribution if your income is more than $218,000. No contribution is allowed if your joint MAGI is over $228,000 in 2023.

3. When can I contribute to a Roth IRA?
According to the IRS, you can make IRA contributions until the tax filing deadline. For 2023, you can fund your ROTH IRA or Traditional IRA until April 15, 2024, the deadline for filing your 2023 tax return.

4. Is there an income limit before I can contribute?

While a Roth IRA is one of the best means for ordinary Americans to build a fortune tax-free, it is not without limitations:

→ Only earned income can be contributed to the fund. Earned income refers to salaries, wages, commissions, tips, etc.

→ If your tax filing status is single, a head of household, or married, filing separately, your 2023 modified adjusted gross income (MAGI) must not exceed $153,000.

→ If you are married and filing taxes jointly, your 2023 MAGI must be less than $228,000.

5. Can a creditor come after money in my Roth IRA?
Unlike your employer-sponsored retirement accounts, such as the 401(k), 403(b), and 457(b) accounts, which generally enjoy protection from creditors, the IRA and Roth IRA offer limited protection from creditors. In a bankruptcy proceeding, the money in your Roth IRA or traditional IRA is exempted from creditors up to $1,363,800. In addition, some states provide additional layers of protection for your IRA and Roth IRA. However, other states, including Nebraska, Georgia, Maine, and California, do not protect Roth IRAs (although these states provide some creditor protection to traditional IRAs). Check your state of residence so you can appropriately assess your risk.

ROTH IRA AND REQUIRED MINIMUM DISTRIBUTIONS

A Required Minimum Distribution (RMD) is the minimum amount of money required by law to be withdrawn or taken out yearly by the owner of a traditional IRA, SEP IRA, or employer-sponsored tax-deferred account, such as 401(k), 403(b), or 457(b), starting at the age of 72. Note that the RMD does not apply to Roth IRAs, so you can leave your money in your Roth IRA to grow by compounded returns when you're 72 and beyond.

TRADITIONAL IRA

A Traditional IRA is an individual retirement account, similar to ROTH, but you contribute to the account with money before taxes are taken out. Your contribution to a traditional IRA is tax-deductible. Traditional IRA lowers your income to be taxed. With a Roth IRA, you contribute money after the tax is taken out. You pay a 10% penalty if you withdraw money from an IRA before 59 ½ years old.

However, in Traditional IRA, you pay taxes on the money you withdraw regardless of your age at the time of your withdrawal. You will be required to withdraw money (the required minimum distribution or RMD) from the Traditional IRA account at age 72, whether you need the money or not.

MAXIMUM CONTRIBUTION TO TRADITIONAL IRA

For 2023, the contribution limit to TRADITIONAL IRA (like a ROTH IRA) is $6,500. If you are 50 years old or over, you can add an extra $1,000, known as a catch-up contribution, for a total of $7,500 in one year. Depending on your income, work retirement participation, and tax-filing status, your IRA contribution is deductible from your taxable income.

In short, your ability to deduct your contribution from your taxable income depends on the following factors, namely:

1. Your tax filing status

2. Your yearly Modified Adjusted Gross Income or MAGI

3. Participation in your employer-sponsored retirement account. So consult with your tax advisor or financial planner.

For illustration purposes, here is an example for the Year 2023:

Filing Status:	Income	Deduction
Single or Head of Household and participant in workplace retirement plan	Income is $73,000 or less	Full Deduction
	More than $73,00 but less than $83,000	Partial Deduction
	Income is $83,000 or more	No deduction is allowed

Filing Status:	Income	Deduction
Married, filing jointly and participant in workplace retirement plan	$116,000 or less	Full Deduction
	More than $116,000 but less than $136,000.	A partial deduction is allowed
	for $136,000 or more	No deduction is allowed
Married filing jointly and spouse is covered by Retirement Plan	Income is less than $218,000	Full deduction
	More than $218,000 but less than $228,000	Partial deduction
	More than $228,000	No deduction

Take note: Unlike ROTH IRA, with a traditional IRA or regular IRA, you can put in the maximum annual contributions even if you make too much money above the threshold income, regardless of your own or your spouse's participation in an employer-sponsored retirement account. But you may be unable to deduct those contributions from your income for tax purposes. So again, you may not be able to deduct your contribution. Still, the money you contributed to your IRA grows tax-free at a compounded rate until you withdraw it.

IRA WITHDRAWAL VERSUS REQUIRED MINIMUM DISTRIBUTION

An owner of a traditional IRA account is required by US tax law to withdraw a minimum amount of money each year from the account starting at the age of 72, whether they need the money or not. Unlike the owner of a Roth IRA, the owner of a traditional IRA account must withdraw the required minimum amount of money from the account. If the account holder fails to draw the RMD money, a 50% excise tax can be imposed on the amount required to be withdrawn from the account.

EXAMPLE:
Dr. Workhorse is 72 ½ years old. He receives $2,700 monthly from Social Security, $3,500 as a pension from his previous employer, and $2,000 monthly dividends from his investments. His wife receives roughly $2,300 from Social Security and a $1,700 monthly pension from her previous employer. The Workhorses think their combined monthly income is more than enough for their overall expenses. In addition, the Workhorse couple has $2,000,000 in their combined 401k and Traditional IRA accounts.

Dr. Workhorse and his wife will be required to withdraw from their IRA and 401k each year, starting at age 72, to meet the RMD imposed by law. Assuming the couple must withdraw $100,000 from their IRA and 401(k) to satisfy the RMD. If they fail, they will pay a 50% excise tax or penalty on the $100,000, the minimum amount they were unable to withdraw.

Take note: If you are reading this book and you think the RMD applies to you, seek the advice of a financial planner or tax adviser for further information.

ROTH IRA VERSUS TRADITIONAL IRA: WHICH IS BETTER?

Whether a Roth or traditional IRA is best depends on your current financial situation and expected income level. For example, ROTH is better if your future income will go up from the proceeds of your employer pension, including your 401(k), 403(b), or 457(b), in addition to income from Social Security and other investments. Roth is better because the money you will eventually withdraw from your Roth will be tax-free. But suppose your future income is lower than your current income; in that case, it is better to contribute to a regular IRA to reduce your taxable income today.

I strongly recommend you consult a financial adviser who can evaluate your situation and tailor an appropriate financial plan.

. This book provides general information to develop your financial strategy and make wiser decisions with better financial outcomes. This book is not intended to replace professional advice specific to you.

Chapter 19

LEVERAGE WEALTH THROUGH LIFE INSURANCE

"If a child, a spouse, a life partner, or a parent depends on you and your income, you need life insurance."

SUZE ORMAN

A life insurance policy is a strategic financial planning tool that allows you to leave a fortune tax-free to your dependents. Do you have enough insurance coverage? Did you set up your policy with a clear understanding of your insurance's value or how it fits into your overall financial planning besides the vague idea that it replaces your income upon your death?

Life insurance remains an uninteresting area of financial planning among healthcare workers. For an agent presenting the topic of insurance, healthcare workers are among the most boring audiences.

As of 2022, about 106,000,000 adult Americans are without or have insufficient life insurance coverage based on the 2022 Insurance Barometer Study performed by LMRA (Life Insurance Marketing and Research Association). A trend shows that people without life insurance or no adequate coverage continue to increase compared to previous years.

One time, I was doing rounds in the ICU as a nursing supervisor when the monitor tech passed the phone to me. The line was choppy; I only heard, "Nurse, I just want to ask my dad where he kept his insurance policy." She hung up before I could verify the patient she was trying to contact. I met the caller, Juliana, when she showed up at the hospital later in my shift. She told me that a particular company wanted to pay her father 75% of the value of his life insurance so that her father and the family could use the money while he was still alive. It is a viatical settlement, another life insurance advantage that can be tapped as a source of emergency funds while the insured is still alive.

In this chapter, you will learn the importance of life insurance as part of your overall financial planning strategy.

INSURANCE: YOU NEED IT!

Sometime in 2009, during the last financial recession, our friend Ryan lost his job with a construction company. It was one of the sectors worst hit by the recession. Ryan finally took a maintenance job in the hospital. But his new job paid him almost 50% less than his previous job as a construction site lead. Even after he found new employment, Ryan was worried about his family falling into hard times. To save money, Ryan canceled their cable, internet, and any other monthly expenses they could. He decided to cancel his whole life policy with a monthly premium of $115; Ryan only saw the cash value of $30,000. At first, he was adamant that he should wait to cancel his insurance policy until his new one took effect. But it was the holiday season, and he needed the money from the cash value. Ryan surrendered the policy in December 2009 before he had a chance to comply with the medical requirements for the new policy.

The following month, January 2010, before he was able to complete his health screening requirements, Ryan died from cardiac arrest. He was 51 years old. Ryan left behind a 48-year-old wife, Angie, who works in the local hospital medical records. They have four kids, ages 18, 11, 7, and 5. It was already a financially difficult time for everyone in the family, but their situation was more tragic from the sudden death of a breadwinner who left nothing for his dependents.

When hard times fall on families—such as when the breadwinner loses a job or suffers a debilitating injury or sickness—and bills are piling up, the next thing that usually comes to mind for many is to cancel their life insurance policy, especially when it has a cash value. It is understandable.

What should you do if you find yourself in a similar situation? Why you want to cancel your policy and how you want to cancel it is your call, but when to cancel your policy is a matter of sound judgment and prudence. You must wait to cancel your existing policy until the new one takes effect. No arguments!

PRUDENT BREADWINNERS HAVE LIFE INSURANCE

According to Merriam-Webster's dictionary, a prudent person observes caution or circumspection or exercises sound judgment in the use of resources. How does this relate to insurance? A sensible man or woman with dependents will take out a life insurance policy to ensure that if something were to happen to him or her, the dependents would have sufficient funds: to finish their studies, pay for transportation, pay the home mortgage or rent, and meet other necessary expenses. It must be a part of sound financial planning.

POLICY: A SACRED CONTRACT

A life insurance policy is a sacred contract between you and your insurance company. When an event or condition happens as stipulated in the agreement, the company will pay the designated persons as beneficiaries of the policy amount. Face Value is the amount of the policy or the amount of money stated in the insurance policy to be paid by the Insurance company in favor of the beneficiaries upon the death of the insured. The money you pay the insurance company monthly or quarterly to maintain your insurance is called the premium.

Even a provision in your Will cannot trump the terms of the policy or change the persons you named as its beneficiaries.

INSURANCE PROCEEDS ARE TAX-FREE

Life insurance must be a major component of the sound financial planning of the family. A life insurance policy can be a strategic tool to transfer wealth or enrich the beneficiaries upon the insured's death. Many financial experts claim that insurance is one of the cornerstones of financial planning. Because the policy proceeds (money) paid to the designated beneficiaries are tax-free: these proceeds can cover or pay for any estate taxes. The estate will be transferred to the beneficiaries—usually the family of the person who died—intact, without the need to sell any part of the estate just to pay taxes or fees. That's why rich people consider insurance a part of their family's financial strategy.

Rich people also consider insurance a good investment, so they pay for the appropriate amount of coverage. Unfortunately, many people view insurance as a monthly burden; if they do insure themselves, they tend to take out insufficient coverage. Rich people look at the future, so they look at life insurance as a valuable future gift for their loved ones by paying a small amount of money in the form of a monthly premium. The rich accept the risk and uncertainty of life, but they take strategic measures to mitigate that risk through insurance whenever possible. Unfortunately, many people know and accept the risk but leave that risk to fate or surrender to it.

LEVERAGE

Life insurance is a type of leverage. Leverage refers to a means or strategy used to reinforce or multiply the effects of an action and increase its productivity. A lever can be a device like a pulley, a pill crusher, or a can opener, where a small amount of force enables you to crush a pill or open a can. By using a device or instrument as a lever, a small effort can produce a more significant result or achieve an exponential value.

Regarding finances, debt or insurance can be used as a lever. Using debt, you can buy a house by paying an affordable monthly mortgage. You can attend college, without paying a lump sum, just using a student loan. And by taking out life insurance, you can pay a small monthly premium to ensure that when you die, your beneficiaries will receive a sum of money much greater than the total cost of premiums.

If you cannot set aside a million dollars in your lifetime, at least in death, you can achieve a million or more for your loved ones through insurance proceeds.

EXAMPLE:

John, an Assistant Physical Therapist, is 42 years old. He took out a $500,000 25-year term life insurance policy and pays a $70 monthly premium. By paying an affordable monthly premium, he uses the insurance policy as a lever to allow him to leave $500,000 for his beneficiaries to replace his income upon his death.

TERM INSURANCE

Term insurance prescribes a specific period for the risk (i.e., death) to occur for the insurance company to pay beneficiaries the face value of the policy. The specified period (term duration) can be 20 years, 25 years, or longer. For the beneficiary to receive the policy's proceeds, the risk insured must happen within that period. The biggest attraction of term insurance is its lower premium and ability to help you achieve the purpose for which you insured your life: protecting your loved ones from financial loss by paying a small amount of money.

EXAMPLE:

Marco, a 40-year-old psychiatric technician, has two sons, ages 9 and 11. He took out a 20-year term insurance policy for $400,000 and pays a $75 monthly premium; his total premium for 12 months is $900, and his total premium for 20 years is $18,000. The term policy will expire when Marco is 60 years old. By then, his two kids will be 31 and 29. Twenty years from now, Marco's two sons will likely have graduated from college and be fully employed. As a result, they will not be dependent on Marco for support when the policy term expires 20 years from today.

LADDERING TERM INSURANCE

You buy Term Insurance at different times to mature at different times say every five (5) years. Example: you take a 20-year - Term Policy every 5 years which will mature at a 5-year interval. This is another way to leverage Term Insurance Policy by laddering the policies in your life. In her article "A Guide to Life Insurance Laddering," financial expert Amanda Dixon explains, "Ladders have rungs. So in the financial sense, when you build a ladder, you're creating rungs by purchasing different versions of the same item at different times. In other words, you can add multiple types of a single financial product to your portfolio so that your investments mature at different rates."[26]

EXAMPLE:

At age 40, Peter took out a 20-year term policy with a face value of $400,000. It will expire when Peter is 60 years old. Peter pays a $70 monthly premium. He has two kids, 10-year-old Johnny, and 12-year-old Megan.

After five years, at age 45, Peter realized he was getting older and decided to take out an additional 20-year term

---

26   Dixon, "A Guide to Life Insurance Laddering."

policy at a lower face value of, say, $350,000. This policy will expire when Peter is 65. By the time the policy expires, Peter's youngest child is 35, and his oldest is 37. After 5 more years, at age 50, Peter can take out another 20-year term insurance policy with a face value of $250,000. At this time, Johnny is 20 years old, and Megan is 22. So when this latest term policy expires, Peter will be 70, his oldest child will be 42, and the youngest will be 40.

That is an example of laddering term insurance policies. When Peter turns 60 and his first insurance policy expires, he is still covered by his later two policies for a total of $600,000. And before he turns 60, for example, at age 55 or 57—if Peter is still healthy or insurable, he can obtain another policy for a $250,000 face value if he wants to.

One key benefit of laddering term insurance is that the premiums for term insurance remain low. You may be surprised to learn that Peter's total premium payments for all these various term policies may still be cheaper than the premium he might have paid for a whole life or cash-value insurance policy of the same face value.

Financial experts tend to recommend term insurance because the premiums are so much lower and because the purpose for which insurance is necessary can be served just as well through term insurance. But be careful—insurance sales associates will prod you for a cash-value insurance policy like universal or whole life. So as you sit with the insurance rep, remember it's your money and your choice.

CASH VALUE INSURANCE

Cash value insurance is an insurance policy with the added feature of using a portion of the monthly premium for investments that generate gains or dividends. The interest or investment gain grows on a tax-deferred basis. Two examples of cash-value life insurance are universal life insurance and whole life insurance. Cash value refers to the amount of money generated or earned from the investment portion of the cash value insurance policy. The policy owner can borrow money from the cash value or get the entire value by surrendering his life policy. When he abandons the policy, the insurance company will cancel it.

EXAMPLE:

Dr. Conrad, 45 years old, took out an insurance policy with a face value of $250,000. He pays a $125 monthly premium, three or more times higher than he would have paid for term insurance of the same face value. The investment portion of the policy has earned interest of $10,000 after five years. That $10,000 is the cash value, also called residual cash value. If the investment portion of the insurance keeps growing every year, the cash value will also increase. Thus, after another five years, that cash value grows from $10,000 to $15,000. The cash value remains tax deferred.

HIGHER PREMIUM FOR CASH VALUE INSURANCE

The insured will pay a higher monthly premium for a whole life or universal life insurance policy than term insurance, which has no investment feature for generating interest or gains. The difference between term and whole life insurance payments is usually significant enough to be invested in a mutual fund, 401(k), 403(b), or IRA.

This is how your monthly premium for cash value insurance is allocated:

→ One portion of your premium goes to the investment to generate the gains or interest.

→ Another portion of your premium goes to the actual cost of insuring the person.

→ The final portion of your premium is used to pay administrative fees and other expenses to maintain your insurance.

EXAMPLE:

John Deer, a CNA, took out a universal life insurance policy for $300,000. The $300,000 is the policy's amount or face value. Because the policy taken out by John Deer is universal life, the premium every month is much higher than term insurance. However, the policy will generate interest or earnings. Assuming the insurance company's investment remains profitable for ten years, the policy might have generated $5,000 by then. That $5,000 is the cash value. If John holds on to the policy for another 20 years and the investment returns remain sound, the cash value could go as high as $25,000 or more.

CASH VALUE Q &A:

Let's look at a few common questions about the cash value of insurance policies.

1. Who will get the cash value upon the insured's death?

In the example above, if John dies and his whole life or universal life insurance policy has a face value of $300,000 and a $50,000 cash value, the cash value will go to the insurance company, not to John's beneficiaries. John's beneficiaries will only receive the insurance face value, the amount of which was determined when the insured first took out the policy.

Generally, the insurance company will absorb the cash value unless you pay an extra premium or there is a rider or added provision in the policy that your beneficiary will receive both the cash value and the face amount of the policy.

2. Can I borrow money from my policy's cash value?
Yes, you can borrow as much as 90 to 95% of the cash value in your policy. Why only 90 percent or 95%? So that there is money left to cover or pay your premium if you cannot pay on time. This is an important safeguard that will prevent your insurance from lapsing.

3. Do I need a good credit score to borrow from cash value?

This is another benefit: as the policyholder, you don't need a good credit score to borrow money from your cash value policy. In addition, the interest rate is usually between

4 and 6%, depending on the policy term, which is much lower than your bank's credit card rate.

4. What happens to me if I do not pay the cash value I borrowed?

If you do not repay the borrowed money, it will accumulate more interest when you do not pay. Upon your death, the money you borrowed plus any interest earned will be deducted from the face value of your policy. As a result, your insurance beneficiaries will receive less than the figure stated at the face value of the policy.

EXAMPLE:
Donald took out whole life insurance for $300,000. After ten years, the cash value is $30,000. He decided to borrow $20,000 but never paid back the money from the cash value. After 15 years, the interest accumulated is almost $10,000. This $10,000 interest was added to the $20,000 that Donald borrowed for a total of $30,000. When Donald dies, his beneficiaries will get the face amount of the policy but minus the $30,000.

5. Can I withdraw my cash value without paying taxes?

Yes, you can withdraw the full cash value in the policy without paying taxes, provided that the cash value equals the total premium you paid to the policy. Any excess amount over the total premium paid is taxable income.

However, when you withdraw the cash value, you lose the chicken that lays the golden egg. You lose the insurance that generates the cash value when you surrender the policy to the company.

SUMMARY

Life insurance is not about the death of the policyholder; it is about the life and the quality of life of those who will be left behind. A prudent person with dependents will never cross the street without an insurance policy that will replace his income and provide stability to the dependents in the event of sudden death. Death is certain. Never cancel a life policy until you've replaced it with another fully effective policy.

Remember, your insurance policy is your leverage or device to leave a significant amount of money to your loved ones by paying a small amount every month. Your dependents will receive more than your total insurance premiums if something happens to you.

A term policy can be three times cheaper than a whole or universal life policy. But both Whole life and Universal policy generate a cash value. Therefore, universal life or whole life insurance is also called a cash value insurance policy.

The difference in premium can be invested in a mutual fund, which will likely generate more than the insurance's cash value. Upon the insured's death, the cash value will go to the insurance company unless there is a condition that the cash value will go to the beneficiaries (and the policyholder will pay an added premium for that).

Nowadays, you can find settlement companies that buy life insurance policies held by people with terminal illnesses and similar conditions for a fraction of these policies' face value. The insured can sell the life insurance policy to such a company and use the proceeds without waiting for the insured's death.

ONE WORD OF CAUTION:

When hard times fall on families, monthly insurance premiums are often on the chopping block when cutting costs and expenses. Is there a more tragic situation than losing a loved one, the family's breadwinner, without any funds to replace their income? Therefore, never cancel a policy until it is replaced and the new policy is fully effective. A prudent person will always have a life policy for dependents.

Chapter 20

ANATOMY OF DEBT

"Live within your means, never be in debt, and by husbanding your money, you can always lay it out well."

ANDREW JACKSON

Americans love credit cards, health care workers included. And who can blame them? After all, it is the most accessible means of obtaining the things we want and giving us instant gratification.

Credit cards are, without a doubt, easy and convenient. They bring instant satisfaction. However, this convenience comes with costly consequences.

CREDIT CARD ABUSE

People need to learn how to use credit cards. People abuse credit cards. Abuse occurs any time something is overused, mistreated, or improperly handled contrary to its natural value or purpose. You abuse plastic when you swipe it unwisely or for an unreasonable purpose that results in a financial burden.

You carry a burden whenever you are indebted to another person or a corporation. The responsibility remains on your shoulders — and enshrined in a document, monthly bill, or statement that shows the degree to which you are indebted.

Debt is alright. It is an economic tool that has been employed since time immemorial to obtain the goods or services of another person on the promise that payment will be paid at a later time or in installments. It is a time-tested financial tool. However, the unwise use of debt or borrowing destroys your finances.

GOOD AND BAD DEBT

There is such a thing as good and bad debt. Good debt is the kind that results from leverage, such as when you borrow money for something you know will bring greater value than the cost of the debt itself. For example, you took a $50,000 Student loan to finish school that will give you a college degree, diploma, or vocational skills, which opens opportunities for a high-paying job or lucrative position.

A low-interest mortgage is another example of good debt because you borrow from the bank to buy a house, which provides shelter and appreciation in value or equity. The house builds equity as it increases in value, and you pay down the loan. Equity is your ownership. The mortgage interest is tax deductible. Additionally, many homeowners rent out their houses as a source of revenue.

EXAMPLE:

Mr. Cool is a facility administrator whose position includes the authority to purchase vehicles for his facility. He approved the purchase of a Mercedes-Benz Sprinter

Van on credit at 3.5% interest. He spent $11,700 more than he would have on a competing brand in the market. Mr. Cool proudly reported to corporate that he purchased the van at 1% lower than the listed initially 4.5%. He intended to provide rides to the facility residents when they needed to be picked up or discharged home. He reported that he selected the brand to impress the community as a marketing tool.

After a month, Mr. Cool finds himself in the noodle house, applying for a job.

Mr. Cool's decision raises a few questions. Does the company's marketing strategy require the purchase of a Mercedes, or are there any other effective marketing strategies the company can use to impress? Are other cost-effective vehicles also providing a safe, comfortable ride benefitting the clients? In practice, do we recognize ourselves in Mr. Cool in how we have incurred debts or used credit? Credit card debt is bad debt that should be avoided. But can a good debt turn into a bad debt?

Take note: Even using good debt as leverage can become a bad experience if we fail to attain the result. Let's face it: student loans are always a burden. But spending $75,000 on two-year graduate studies in music, where income growth is practically zero, turns a good debt leverage into a bad debt.

THE ANATOMY OF DEBT

A closer look at the anatomy of debt reveals that we buy on credit because we do not have cash or refuse to shell out cash at the time of the transaction. You might have the means to pay for that new smartphone, dress, or concert ticket. But if that money is set aside or intended for other purposes, you still do not have enough cash for payment. Also, the items or objects we usually bought on credit caught our fancy. We initially thought we could afford to pay at the end of the month, but we ended up not doing so.

One small debt on top of the other small ones until they piled to become a mountain. This is how credit card debts are structured.

Think about it: a quick look back at our experiences will reveal that we accumulate debt on the card, not because of poor choices but because of impulsive and poor decisions. If you see something in the mall that readily attracts you to buy, and you don't have enough cash to cover it, walk out. Most of the time, you will never think about the item again, and your finances will be stronger because of your restraint.

Of course, some people charge their transactions on credit (cards) for convenience, even if they are flush with cash, then immediately pay off their balance. This chapter will not address that practice; instead, it will look at how to avoid debt entirely.

DEBT IS A MORAL AND LEGAL OBLIGATION

There's no other way to look at it: debt is an obligation. A person who borrows money is called a debtor, and the person or company who lends the fund or credit is a creditor. Debt exacts both a legal and a moral duty from the debtor to pay back the creditor in full, plus interest. Of course, there are mechanisms by which you can dispense your legal obligation to pay your debt. Still, you will always be morally obligated to repay the person or company who extended you the credit.

Never borrow with the promise of repaying your debts if you know you do not have or will not have the ability—or the willingness and intention —to follow through on your promise. That is fraud and dishonesty and a recipe for remaining poor.

While the debtor cannot be imprisoned in the absence of fraud in obtaining the credit, the creditor can always file a civil action or lawsuit in court to oblige the debtor to pay the amount borrowed, plus any interest and other costs or damages incurred by the creditor such as attorney's fees and other legal expenses. As you can see, we use credit for the things and services we need, desire, or want due to our lifestyle. So, to minimize your credit card debt, only use this device to purchase items or services you need, and only take on debt you know you can and will repay.

PAY YOUR CREDIT CARD: IT'S AN OBLIGATION

When you cannot (or choose not to) pay your credit card or other debts by the due date, your creditor will give you a grace period, typically 30 days, during which you can still pay your bill without penalty. After that grace period, the creditor will begin charging you late fees and additional interest. Likewise, your creditor will submit your account to a collection agency, a third person, or a company that will do nothing but torment you psychologically to execute what they know best: collecting from you. Meanwhile, your credit score suffers.

Credit cards are the worst form of incurring debt. Credit card debt can stifle, inhibit, and even paralyze financial growth. Pay it as fast as you can possibly do.

Consider this: credit card companies—including the one issued by your favorite bank —charge a whopping 16 to 21% rate of interest and still penalizes you with $35 late fees, and yet your bank only gives you 1.5% interest on the money you lend them as a depositor. So when you deposit your money in your neighborhood bank, you are a creditor, and your bank is a debtor; that is your relationship with that bank. But the table is turned when the same bank is milking you as high as 23% when you use their credit card.

So what should you do? First, you do what you can to make your life more bearable with the bank that issues your credit card.. Next, call the bank or credit union and respectfully ask the representative to lower the interest rate they charge you. Next, call the credit card company and do likewise. Ask to speak with someone in the company who can lower your interest rate. Finally, tell your bank you will pull out your deposit unless it reduces the interest on credit cards. It works more often than you might think!

ATTACK ONE CREDIT CARD WITH ANOTHER CREDIT CARD

What if your credit card debt burden has reached a level that requires critical intervention? Take a deep breath, in and out. Calm down. Do not think of applying for court relief through bankruptcy; that should be your last resort. Instead, apply for promotional or teaser credit cards that offer 0% (as in no interest) for 12 to 18 months.

Just as the happy leaves of summer start to fall, the offers of 0% interest from credit card companies start to fill mailboxes in autumn and continue to winter—just in time for big holidays spending during Thanksgiving, Christmas, and New Year. Grab this opportunity! These zero-interest offers can temporarily relieve your pains.

By transferring your credit card balances to these promotional cards with teaser rates, you will save money on interest, even if you pay a transfer fee of 3% (compared to your current interest of 17 to 23%).

To use this strategy to your advantage, follow these steps:

1. Look into different credit cards and compare their interest rates and the length of time you will pay zero or deferred interest. Check their rewards points.

2. Calculate the transfer fee or cash advance fee offered by the new cards (typically 3% of the amount you want to transfer or charge to the new card).

3. Pay off the balance on the card-carrying higher interest and charges with your new promo cards. If you want to cancel or terminate your other credit cards, keep the oldest card or account open.

By taking these steps, you will effectively pause racking up interest on your credit card debt. Then, after the expiration period of 0% interest, apply for the new teaser rate card and repeat this strategy.

Take note: Some credit cards offer 0% interest as a promotional or teaser rate for up to 18 months. It seems great on paper, but it can have terrible financial consequences if you do not pay what you owe by the end of the promotional period.

DEFERRED INTEREST:

Simply put, you do not pay any interest on your credit card balance from your purchases during the promotional period, provided you pay all your balance before that period expires; otherwise, you will pay the interest deferred starting from the time you use your credit card.

EXAMPLE:

Donald signed up for a new credit card offered by his bank. It gives a deferred interest for 18 months if he pays the entire amount within the grace period. After the promotional period, the interest rate will jump to 24%. At its highest point, Donald's total credit card balance was $5,000, but at the end of 18 months, he had gotten that balance down to $1,500.

Question: Assuming that the interest deferred is $1,000 on the credit card, how much does Donald owe?

ANSWER: The deferred interest will be calculated by adding it to the remaining balance at the end of the promotion period. Donald (assume) owes a total of $2,500 at 24%. With the deferred interest, Donald does not have to pay any interest during the grace period. But if he cannot pay or chooses not to pay the entire balance during the 18-month promotional period, all the unpaid interest—from the first time he charged something on the credit card—will be added to the remaining balance at the end of the 18 months. Unfortunately for Donald, this interest is calculated based on the balance he borrowed or owed each month from when he made the first purchase or since the first time he charged a purchase to the card.

CONSIDER THIS: Contrary to what many financial advisers or financial planners say, if you cannot avoid that big ticketed kitchen appliance that you want to pay in 24 or 36 months, and the credit card charges a higher interest rate, consider borrowing from you retirement account such as 401k 0r 403b. Yes, check it out. Because the money you pay monthly in interest, aside from the principal, goes to your fund. By charging your purchase to a credit card, the money you pay in interest (assuming 23%) goes to your credit card company. Even if your retirement account (considering it charges you the same 23%), at least the money goes back to your account. You did not lose much in terms of investment return on the amount you borrowed as you avoided paying interest to the credit card company. Pay what you borrow from your retirement account to avoid taxes and penalties.

IF YOU CANNOT AVOID IT, SELECT THE BEST

I'm not too fond of Credit Cards. But if you cannot avoid one, let me tell you: get the best card. The best credit card choices are those offering reward points and freebies. When I say points, I mean those cards that reward you with a certain percentage of your charge. Some cards also give you points that can be converted into travel tickets, hotel accommodations, and gifts. Of course, pay what you are charged by the due date.

My daughter, Katrina, charged her $1600 trip to Asia plane ticket to her card. But after two days, she earned

$105.00 and some change as a reward. She said she pays her card monthly to avoid being charged interest.

I don't want to talk more about credit cards. I said I do not like to use it anyway. But I have one in an emergency where you need to use it rather than cash.

DEBT AS A LEVER

Debt is a positive financial strategy if used to carry out an investment or undertaking that will result in more benefits than the cost of debts. By cost of debt, I mean the principal to be paid plus the interest and other charges. Debt can also be a powerful financial tool as a lever.

But what is this lever that we heard or read? First, look at how a pulley is used as a lever. With this simple device, you can lift a heavy object with less force or effort, which results in greater efficiency. Without a pulley as your lever, you would need to exert much more energy and effort to lift that object.

Unbeknownst to many of us, when you use a bank loan to finance your house purchase, you use debt as leverage: the mortgage on your house is employed to acquire the house you could not otherwise afford to pay for cash. In the meantime, the home provides shelter to your family and protection from the elements. It also gives you equity every time you pay the monthly mortgage and its value increases.

Additionally, when you borrow from your equity line of credit that charges you 3.8% to pay off a credit card debt that charges you 19%, you are using your home equity line of credit as leverage to facilitate the payment of your more onerous high-interest-rate credit card. You are using another debt as a lever to avoid paying more interest. Borrowing from your equity line of credit is a good debt. You can leverage it to release some of the assets in your house so you can use them to pay other onerous or high-interest debts.

WARNING: You must pay back your home equity in the period specified for your equity line of credit, or you will lose your house. You will not lose your house for not paying your credit cards. But you will lose your house for not paying the home equity line of credit where you took money to pay your credit cards and other debts.

SUMMARY

→ Use credit cards for convenience, documentation purposes, or online purchases that you have the readiness and ability to pay in a few short months. Further, use a credit card or debt for items that build value, not for groceries or consumables, unless it is your last resort. Today, banks and groceries encourage you to do it —but do you want to be paying for those "consumables" long after they have already been flushed down the drain? If you use a card for daily purchases for reward points, pay your balance in full by the end of each month.

→ Use teaser or promotional rates of 0% to transfer and unburden yourself of high-interest credit cards or other debts, but be mindful of the expiration date for those promotional interest rates. Try to pay more than the minimum amount required or approximate your monthly payment so that by the expiration of the promotional period, you are fully paid or at least have a lower balance which you can transfer again to another credit card.

Note: failure to pay in full by the end of the grace period or before the promo period expires will leave you with high credit card interest rates—usually 22 to 25%—on the entire amount you used or transferred, including accrued interest counted back from the time of your transaction (and not from the time of the expiration of the promo period). If you cannot pay your balance in full before the end of the grace period, transfer it to another card offering 0% interest.

→ Use debt as a lever, but consider the cost of that debt or credit in relation to the risk, benefits, profitability, and opportunity you could derive from other investments by using the debt proceeds.

Chapter 21

SAVING FOR COLLEGE

"If you think education is expensive, try ignorance."

ANDY MCINTYRE

The university president finally declared, "You are now grad-uates!" Big applause rose from the graduates, their families, and guests. People in the hall were clapping and screaming in joy. We were there—we were part of it. It was in June of 2018 when Katrina, our youngest daughter, graduated from college. My wife and I were overwhelmed with joy. We had finally handed to our youngest family member the legacy of a college education without the burden of student loans.

Parents dream of seeing children graduate from college or trade school equipped with marketable skills and knowl-edge. But behind those dreams, the reality of pursuing that highly coveted college or vocational diploma is getting uglier. The tuition fees and related college expenses are rising so quickly that parents and students cannot keep up. The only option is to take a student loan. It is disheartening to see so many young adults starting their professional lives burdened with student loan debt when it could have been avoided or mitigated.

That's right: there is a sure ticket to fund the college tuition expenses of a child without requiring burdensome student loans. It would help if you started now because time is your secret ticket. Don't get me wrong: student loans exist to help students and parents who cannot access a college education. However, I wish our children in America—most of them as young as 21 years of age—would graduate without upward of $55,000 in student loan debt. I wish they could leave the safe confines of their dormitories and college campuses to start a new life focused solely on their new world.

There is no reason that your child should take a student loan just because so many others are doing the same. If parents have a way to fund their child's college education in advance through a 529 plan, it is unfair to wait for a child to turn 18 and let them carry the burden of student loan debts.

THE PSYCHOSOCIAL BURDEN OF STUDENT LOANS

If you are the parents, take note — it is not only the figures of their loans that weigh on the shoulders of our daughters and sons today; the emotional, social, and psychological consequences of the college loan are a heavier burden to bear. Student loans have unintended but immediate social and psychological effects on your children. It contributes to anxiety and depression among borrowers, especially if they are forced to stay at their current jobs and have limited options but to stay and deal with abusive managers and lousy supervisors. That is the unfortunate truth in a tight job market: workers have no choice but to remain in toxic workplaces because they must pay their massive student loans on top of other bills.

Student loan debt affects young adults' ability to set aside money for their future. Student loans affect the ability to buy a car or a house. The burden of student loans even limits them from making important life decisions like marrying or having a child. Student loan debt is a severe financial burden that cannot be discharged through bankruptcy. Failure to pay their federal student loan will result in your child's future salary and tax refund money being garnished.

As a parent, you do not want your children to suffer this fate when you can take steps now to lessen their burden through proper planning and budgeting. With this proven strategy for managing your money, parents can finance their children's college education without adversely impacting their ability to build financial security in retirement.

THE HARD TRUTH OF STUDENT LOANS

The statistics on student loans are alarming. In her August 2021 article "Student Loan Debt Statistics," Melanie Hanson reported, "US student loan debts reached $1.73 trillion in total in 2020. On a national average, each student owes $39,351 on student loans in 2020."[27] First Republic Bank also noted in March 2021 that the total national student loan debts are higher than the total mortgage or automobile loans in the US. Student loans are projected to keep going up.[28]

In contrast, Mark Kantrowitz, a recognized expert on financial aid and publisher, reported in 2018 that among the graduating class of that year, 69% of college students took out student loans. They graduated with an average debt of $29,800, including private and federal debt. Meanwhile, 14% of their parents took out an average of $35,600 in federal

27 Hanson, "Student Loan Debt Statistics."
28 First Republic Bank, "U.S. Student Loan Debt Statistics."

Parent PLUS loans. Nurses and other healthcare workers easily climb up or belong to the middle class because of their household income. Accordingly, they shoulder the weight of student loans.[29]

A study by Jason Houle, a sociology professor from Dartmouth University, shows that middle-class students face a higher student loan debt burden after graduating than other groups. Professor Houle's study found that "children from middle-income families make too much money to qualify for student aid packages, but they do not have the financial means to cover college costs."[30]

According to Michael Stratford in a 2013 article for Inside Higher Ed, Houle's study "found that students from families earning between $40,000 to $59,000 per year racked up 60% more debt than lower-income students and 280% more than their peers whose families earned between $100,000 and $149,000 per year. A similar trend held for more affluent middle-income families earning up to $99,000 annually."[31]

So what can parents do to set their children up for success? Saving early for your child's college and related expenses is a wonderful expression of love and legacy for your children. Your child will enter college as a freshman with less financial stress than others because their parents' smart decisions have prepared their basic campus needs.

We started saving for our children's college tuition fees and college-related expenses through 529 when our oldest

---

29   Saving for College, "Mark Kantrowitz."

30   Danna, "Houle Study: Which Students Have the Most College Loan Debt."

31   Stratford, "Study: Student Debt Squeezes Middle Class the Most."

daughter, Audrey, was already in the first grade. It was earlier for the youngest, Katrina, about a few months old. So, as a parent, if you're wondering what you can do to save for your child's future education, my best answer is to start early and take out a 529 college savings plan.

Opening a 529 plan is one of the most effective strategies for funding your kids' college tuition fees and school-related expenses like books, college housing, and computers. In his book, The Best Way to Save for College, Joseph F. Hurley confirms that 529 plans are the best way to save for their education.[32]

COLLEGE SAVINGS PLAN Q&A

Let's look at a few common questions about 529 college savings plans.

1. WHERE DID 529 PLANS COME FROM?

You can find information about 529 plans in Section 529 of the Internal Revenue Code, which allows for a tax-free savings account for higher education expenses. IRC 529 was added to the Internal Revenue Code via Section 1806 of the Small Business Job Protection Act of 1996.

2. WHAT IS A 529 PLAN?

A 529 plan is a tax-advantaged savings plan designed to encourage saving for future higher education costs. The

---

32   Hurley, *The Best Way to Save for College : A Complete Guide to 529 Plans.*

profits or any gain on the money contributed to the 529 plans are all tax-free. In addition, some States allow tax deductions of the contribution to the 529 Plans. They are legally known as qualified tuition plans. They are sponsored by states, state agencies, or educational institutions and authorized by Section 529 of the Internal Revenue Code. Per the Internal Revenue Code, funds must be spent on "qualified higher education expenses."

3. WHAT EXPENSES QUALIFY FOR PAYMENT WITH A 529 PLAN?

Qualified higher educational expenses (QHEE) include tuition, school-related fees, books, school supplies, and electronic/digital equipment required for the enrollment or attendance of a designated beneficiary who is an eligible student at an eligible educational institution. Generally, an eligible student is a student who attends at least half-time as determined by the institution. The amount of room and board treated as qualified higher education expenses must not exceed the school-prescribed budget allowance for room and board. Costs of necessary special needs services in connection with such enrollment or attendance are also qualified higher education expenses.

4. WHAT ARE THE ESSENTIAL FEATURES OF A 529?

The money saved in a 529 plan account grows tax-free and is exempted from federal and state tax. The money you withdraw is also tax-free, provided that you use that money for qualified higher education related expenses or QHEE.

Any person can contribute to the college or school expenses of the child listed on the 529 accounts. "Any person" means the child's parents, grandparents, aunts, uncles, siblings, and friends. An individual can contribute up to $17,000 to the 529 plan of the beneficiary (up to $34,000 for a married couple) without paying gift taxes.

A 529 plan does not impose an income restriction on the investor or contributor to the fund. To tax the contribution as a gift, any contribution above $17,000 in a year or above $85,000 in 5 years may be subject to a Gift tax.

You can open a 529 Account for your child, grandchild, friend, nephew, niece, or even for yourself as a beneficiary. You can change or replace the beneficiary at any time. It applies if they refuse to go to college or obtain a scholarship award.

Different states, however, have their restrictions on the maximum amount that can be contributed to the 529 plans of the beneficiary:

→ In Georgia, Tennessee, and Mississippi, the total contribution for a child or beneficiary is $235,000.

→ In the states of Idaho, Louisiana, Michigan, New Hampshire, South Carolina, and Washington, the maximum total contribution to a 529 account is $500,000.

→ In New York, the maximum contribution to a 529 account per beneficiary or child is $520,000.

→ In California, the maximum amount that can be contributed is $529,000.

→ Depending on the state of your residence, your contribution to a 529 account may be tax deductible or applied as a tax credit for the year the contribution was made. Please seek your tax adviser for more information.

→ The original child beneficiary can be replaced anytime with another child, or the money in the 529 accounts can be given to another child's qualified educational expenses.

→ The parent or account holder retains control of the fund. As the account owner, you can terminate the fund, withdraw from the fund, or change the beneficiary.

→ Any withdrawal of the fund for purposes other than qualified higher education expenses will result in a 10% penalty, in addition to state and federal income tax, unless the withdrawal is due to death or disability.

→ A 529 account is protected from creditors, meaning no creditors can put their hands on this money. Most states protect or exempt the funds in this account in bankruptcy petitions.

Setting up your child as the beneficiary of a 529 plan is a great way to fund their future education. Consult IRC 25A(b)(3) or a financial adviser familiar with these college savings plans to learn more.

SUMMARY

As parents, we are responsible for educating our children: to acquire knowledge and skills to prepare them to compete in the real world.

Unfortunately, student loan debt is like a fishing sinker, deeply weighing our children's social and psychological well-being. It affected their life choices and pressured them to work with unsavory bosses or accept jobs to meet their payment due date. Imagine if this is your 22-year-old daughter with $125,000 in student loan debts.

Proper planning and foresight allow educational expenses to be mitigated or funded through a 529 account while saving for retirement. The money you contributed to 529 is tax deductible, depending on the state. It grows tax-free, and you can withdraw the funds, also tax-free, for qualified higher education expenses. It is worth mentioning that the maximum contribution limit to a 529 Plan in favor of a beneficiary can range from $235,000 to as high as $529,000, depending on the state-set limit. As a bonus, your creditors cannot reach the money in your 529 Account.

Chapter 22

THE KARMIC LAW
OF GIVING

"It is in giving that you receive."

SAINT FRANCIS OF ASSISI

You have heard, more than a few times, that to get rich, all you need to do is work hard, acquire as much as you can, invest, and save more. The tighter you squeeze the dollar, the more juice you can get out of it. On the other hand, you have also heard people talk about the value of giving or sharing to others, including charity as a tax strategy. Many believe that generosity is sharing or giving to others those tangibles they can readily spare. In fact, there are more lip services on giving than the actual work. People have vague and different ideas about giving and building wealth. But only a few have truly discovered the Karmic key to the vault of wealth as rewards of generosity.

GIVE TO BE RICH

You may wonder why I included a chapter on generosity as part of this book. This subject is apparently out of place in this book; the idea of giving or sharing is incompatible with wealth and becoming rich, which this book purports to help readers achieve. By all appearances, giving or sharing means a deduction or disposition of something you have. On the other hand, building wealth requires a mindset of acquisition, profit-taking, building values, saving, and investment. Unfortunately, it is a prevailing misconception that charity or generosity has no place in building wealth or becoming rich.

Author Keith Cameron Smith spent two years with rich people for his book, The Top Ten Distinctions Between Millionaires and the Middle Class. He studied and closely observed how these rich people think, their outlook, priorities, and values, including their attitudes toward risk. The author has observed the traits that made them stand out compared to the middle class. In his book, Smith wrote, "Rich people see generosity as a matter of necessity. The middle-class people believe they cannot afford to give. Most millionaires believe in the law of sowing and reaping. Rich people see money as a seed. Millionaires know that if they are generous, they will receive more in return."[33]

THOUGHTS ON GIVING

I met people who practice the virtue of generosity. I could feel the positive energy that draws others to their selflessness. They come from different walks of life. Some own family businesses or shops. Others occupy positions on corporate boards. Many others are fully employed professionals; the rest are ordinary American workers.

My wife and I have experienced the profound rewards of giving. I was inspired to write this chapter not so much because of the joy of giving but because of the sense of reconnection to the core of our humanity and the enriching

---

33   Smith, *The Top 10 Distinctions Between Millionaires and the Middle Class.*

rewards of giving. I do not doubt that generosity and prosperity are ordained by natural design as continuum events. Indeed, there is a metaphysical connection between giving and receiving, just as an intangible connection between generosity and prosperity. By metaphysical connection, I mean that realm of reality that cannot be easily demonstrated by senses or quantified by any means but is comprehensible only as an unbroken phenomenon. It is the same way we understand and accept the natural law of cause and effect. You cannot separate cause from effect. There is no effect without something causing the thing as an effect.

We can quantify the things we have given or shared, but putting a price tag on everything we positively do for others is impossible. Can you measure your intention to help others or tag your price as a community volunteer? Who can quantify the value of your advocacy or your voice to stand up for a cause? Whether or not anyone can put a value on what you have given up, no one can put a tag price on the generosity of your heart. That is why, in the grand scheme of things, the Karmic laws have ordained that the doer of good or evil acts receives an unmeasured wage over and beyond what he has done or given away.

In practical terms, when you give something to others, you deprive yourself of the object or reduce the amount you have. You also deprive yourself of its value and usefulness. On the other hand, the recipient of your good deed is enriched by your deprivation.

OPEN UP YOURSELF BY GIVING UP

When you give, something within your domain opens up when you give up what you have. A space is created in the process. That open space—created by your positive act of giving—attracts positive karmic energy, causing them to flow into that space and refill it. These positive forces enable the giver to rise above his circumstances to accomplish more. In this way, you as the giver, your empty cup will be filled prosperously. The giver will be justly made whole again.

It defies logic that the generous giver would not be made whole while the non-giver would overflow at the brim. A farmer cannot sow one season after another without a season of abundant harvest. It is impossible to only give without receiving. The more you give, the more you must receive. The more you receive, the more you are enriched. That is the universal law of Karma.

UNLOCK PROSPERITY

I believe there is an unwritten law that connects our actions or words to the universe that generates responses of equal or greater intensity. I don't know what it is called. Many people refer to it as Karma. But I only believe in what it ordains. I didn't write this book to persuade you to believe me. In fact, it does not matter to me whether or not you are convinced by what I've written. What I believe in matters, not what you believe or do not believe. I am simply writing from the well of personal experience.

Regardless, I believe that at this very moment, you hold the key to unlock the positive karmic forces of the universe. An act of generosity or an altruistic act is all that matters. The key to prosperity is in your heart. It is the same key used by the most prosperous people throughout generations. It is the same key utilized by those who have unlocked the universe's abundance and left footprints of generosity not washed away by the passing tides of time. Use it to attract the positive forces of the universe.

Generosity is the mother of prosperity, just as the mother to a child. You cannot disrupt or break up the relationship between a mother and the child, nor can you disrupt the metaphysical relationship of generosity and prosperity.

MUTUALITY OF BENEFITS

You don't need to actually give if you do not have one. Your intention to share matters. You must have at least the sincerity of desire or intention to share. That is the mutuality of benefits. You cannot just be an island unto yourself. But as you build value or start to reap from what you have sown, the world must mutually benefit or share from it.

Grab a handful of sand and loosen your hold; you retain quite a bit more in your hand. But grab a handful of the same sand and hold it tight; the grains of sand are slipping through your fingers. That is the natural order of things. You cannot grab and grab more with the claws of desire and self-interest without possibly losing some. Some things must fall back to the universe for others to catch them.

As the poet Maya Angelou said, "I've learned that you should not go through life with catcher's mitts on both hands. You need to be able to throw something back."

When you donate, for example, $100 to a worthy cause, you add value to the organization so they can carry out their advocacy. Likewise, when you give a gratuity to a young woman at the restaurant, you add value to the server who might be working her way to college. When you give $50 or

$500 to your church or any charitable group, you are actually reaching out to enrich the lives of others. The church or charitable organization becomes your medium using its mission and outreach programs. Even those small amounts that you gave to various recipients here and there, in total, become a more significant value.

THE KARMIC LAW ON HUMAN ACTION

Your action has meaning. It sends a message that connects you to the world. It generates a reaction or chain reactions. When you perform a positive action, it attracts a positive response or chain of positive reactions. Conversely, an evil act logically generates an adverse reaction or a chain of negative reactions.

Giving is a specific act with clear universal meaning to the receiver. It is a good act. You cannot think of something good as an effect without thinking of the cause that caused the good thing. That is the chain of causation: one merely reaps what he has sown. But most of the time, the sower reaps more than what he has sown. That is Karma, a universal unwritten law that you attract or draw a reaction or chain reactions depending on the action you perform. You cannot violate the law of Karma without any consequence.

When you give, your body and mind participate in the meaningful experience of unfolding your whole being. The moment you open your hand in the final gesture of generosity, you open yourself to the abundance of the universe. Your positive words and actions are your bridges that connect to the goodwill of the universe. Putting positive words or good deeds creates a good connection. Good connection brings unhampered and clear reactions.

KARMA RETURNS MORE THAN WHAT WAS GIVEN AWAY

Generosity begets generosity. But more than that, generosity also begets prosperity. That is why generosity is often said to be the mother of prosperity. Most of the time, you reap more than what you sow because the good deeds we do for others return more generously. Moreover, good deeds attract the goodwill of people around you.

I was invited to give a commencement speech at a high school graduation in the Philippines in April 2015. I met a graduating student named Karoline, who delivered the valedictory address. This young girl was quite impressive. She carried our hearts away when she narrated her journey through poverty to finish high school. She mentioned her almost six-mile walk every day to school and back home. This story is incredible in America, I thought. At times, she had to go without enough food. But despite these challenges, she made it to the top of all graduating high school seniors.

While Karoline was dedicating one of her school medals to a friend during the valedictory address, she said: "We looked at the same sky and weaved the same dreams. To finish college and become a teacher. This medal is your reward for walking every day for your dream that will remain a dream."

I learned that one evening Karoline's friend was found dead (and raped) while walking a few minutes late behind their group after she passed by the store to pick up a bag of rice from school.

While the students were marching to receive their certificates, I asked Karoline and her mother to meet me and my wife after the graduation ceremony to offer our financial assistance. But they did not show up.

My wife and I drove back to the village the following day to look for Karoline's house. After asking some folks, we finally found their small hut in a remote location outside the village. The house was bare of necessities. Gaping holes in the roof allowed the rain to drop with no hesitation. There was no electricity; two kerosene lamps provided the only light. I wondered how the girl had managed to study and gain such an impressive command of the English language and math.

The mother apologized immediately for not showing up. But then, it was Karoline who admitted, "We were ashamed. We were afraid of what the people would say."

Their poverty and life circumstances had made the mother and daughter timid. Finally, my wife and I offered to send Karoline to college as a freshman. At this time, our youngest daughter, Katrina, was entering college as a freshman. Karoline was not the first kid we assisted in college, but her life circumstances touched us more than the other kids we helped. It could be because Karoline and our daughter, Katrina, were almost the same age and at the same college level.

After her sophomore year, Katrina was accepted into Microsoft's summer internship. Karoline was also accepted as a teaching intern. The following summer, Katrina was again offered a summer internship with Microsoft in Redmond, Washington, as well as another internship opportunity in the field of cybersecurity research from an Ivy League school in Boston. Then, eight months before Katrina graduated, she was offered a job at Microsoft and received a portion of a generous sign-on bonus. Right around that time, Karoline also wrote to us she had met all the requirements to graduate with a degree in education. Today, as I write this book, Karoline is employed as a teacher.

By some unknown design, we were not paying for Katrina's college expenses two years before she graduated. As a result, we saved a good amount of money that could have otherwise been spent on her college tuition fees, dormitory, allowance, and books. Unknown to us, Katrina paid for those things with the money she received as a Microsoft intern.

Karma has a mysterious way of returning the favors you gave to make the world a better place to live. This universal karmic law has a way of repaying you in an amazing fashion. The return delivery may not come straight back to you. Still, it is ultimately returned to enrich the people you deeply care about.

GENEROSITY IS IN THE HEART

There are various ways of giving to express generosity. One day, I asked my wife why we were getting mails from multiple organizations soliciting donations. Mails came from veterans, police, firefighters associations, and even from the Olympics. I found out that my wife had been writing small checks here and there for those random solicitors.

Friends advised us not to give money to these organizations because they were phonies, and out to fool others into giving. I agree that we need to be cautious. But one cannot be genuinely generous by being judgmental of others. It is not for us to judge the sincerity or bad faith of the recipients of our generosity. It is for us to judge whether our act flows from sincerity.

FACES OF GIVING

There are various ways of giving and showing your generosity. You are sharing when you volunteer at your church and community. It is more meaningful if the whole family can volunteer together. No one can value the time you and your family spent as community or church volunteers.

It's generosity when you spend $10 or $20 on chocolate bars or cookies from a colleague for her child's school project. Don't buy just because you want to please your colleague while telling yourself it's a waste of your $20 bucks; by spending that money, you are actually helping to raise funds for the child's school projects.

Buying a glass of lemonade from kids in your neighborhood is also an act of giving. It is not the two dollars or five that matters; it's the lesson you're helping the kids learn, not only about the value of work but also about the rewards of entrepreneurship and self-reliance. This small amount can have a lasting mark on the kids' perspective of the world of business or commerce. Unbeknownst to you, the sale proceeds may be intended to fund a neighborhood project or school program, thus benefiting even more students.

It is giving of yourself when you take a stand and speak up on an issue that no one else dares to raise. It is giving because you draw the fire from your belly and use it to clarify an issue.

You are giving when you put a human face to an abstract idea. You become the voice of both the mute and those who have chosen to be mute out of convenience. It is giving when you lose a part of yourself to give to others.

In contrast, some people are either boneless or luke-warm. They prefer to look in the other direction for fear of losing a favor or falling from "grace" when the situation calls for them to stand up. They like to stand in the middle, indifferent observers, even on issues directly affecting them. Was it Julius Caesar who said," Cowards die many times before their actual death?" The coward passes his shame to his children.

It is an act of generosity when you support the arts, education, sciences, music, and museums. It is an act of giving when you lend voices as advocates for minorities, children, and women. We have heard or read about millionaires who support the arts, music, and museums as patrons. They donate to educational institutions and even lend their names to animal welfare organizations and programs that protect the environment.

Yes, it is an act of thoughtfulness and concern to separate your recyclables from your household waste. Recycling is an acknowledgment of the generosity of Mother Nature and a way of giving back. Recycling enriches and protects the environment from further degradation and pollution. When you advocate for the environment, you give your voice and a human face to protect the ocean, forest, and untamed living creatures. In the end, your good deeds extend to countless people whose livelihood depends on agriculture and other gifts of nature.

MENTAL POVERTY IS BAD COMPANY

Mental poverty is incompatible with generosity. A poverty mindset is a belief, an outlook, and an attitude of inadequacy that is set in the mind. It disposes of a person to tighten his grip or hold on something. You do not want to give because you are worried you will run out or not have enough for tomorrow. Unfortunately, the people around you perceive your attitude. In return, you attract negative energy. This is true because your actions and words, which reflect your mindset, connect your feelings and thoughts to your surroundings. A bad connection generates bad reactions. It is a vicious cycle.

I remember the interesting case of Lucita. She was full of complaints and negative comments about everything, including her patients and co-workers. She has the propensity to unburden her family issues unto unsuspecting peers. Lucita also wanted to be an instant millionaire, as evidenced by her file of old lottery tickets. She went around the Unit and asked her co-workers to chip in for lottery tickets. I refused to join when Lucita was the one buying the lottery tickets — not because I do not play the lottery, but because I believe good Karma does not rush to benefit a stingy hand with contractures.

Lucita often brings to work an Asian rice soup called "lugaw. " Then, like a child, she kept the pot of lugaw under the table to hide it from the rest of us. Lucita distributed it surreptitiously to only three or four people as if she was passing out contraband. Funny thing, even Lucita's favored recipients wondered how much the cup of soup must have cost her that she could not offer it to everyone. Don't get me wrong. She worked hard, except she tends to grab the credit for herself.

THE MINDSET OF GENEROSITY

In contrast to Lucita, we have another colleague, Perla, who loves to bring a pot of her lentil soup to work. When she does, she places the whole pot in plain view with a message: "Scoop it hot." Everybody's free to take a bowl of soup. Perla extends her table to all, regardless of whether she has enough soup. No wonder Perla has such a sunny disposition.

A generous giver shares out of the sincerity of the heart and an attitude of abundance. It is an attitude of abundance when you believe that you don't need more to give or share what you have. That explains why they pass plates without first counting how many are available and provide them regardless of the receiver's culture, color, or creed.

Those who become wealthy and successful in life are generous even during the process of becoming. When they reach the upper ladder, sharing becomes a natural part of them. It is not their net worth or assets that make them generous givers; the abundance in their hearts enables them to give greater and bigger things. Their mindset, values, and sense of purpose in life make them generous. They know that generosity brings them prosperity. That explains why many wealthy people have charitable organizations or foundations to widen their reach. Giving is reciprocating the generosity of the universe. The more they give, the more they receive.

YOUR WORKPLACE: A WORLD'S MICROCOSM

Your workplace is a microcosm of the world. You will notice that you have co-workers readily disposed to share and assist their colleagues. They are the ones who usually bring extra goodies into the workplace and they volunteer to assist others. They have a sunny disposition.

Despite their earnings or income, they tell you they consistently contribute to their 401(k)s or 403(b)s as if telling others to follow. They understand they have a sense of purpose. They tell you how they are involved in the community or in the church. They are engaged in advocacies. They have energy and confidence. They can speak up on issues when all the rest have pressed their mute buttons. They deliver silently without expectation of how much they will see in their paycheck. Their generosity enables them to lend a shoulder to their co-workers.

In contrast, look at some of your other colleagues. They are like blindfolded followers who won't even take a stand on a work issue affecting everyone. When the situation calls for them to volunteer or contribute, they first ask how much they'll be paid or what they'll receive in return. They complain of not having enough despite their income and the hours of work they put in. You can observe them being overly vigilant about what is in their paychecks as if their employer is cheating them.

Indeed, your workplace is a mirror of the big world just as the workers mirror who and what they are outside of the workplace. If they are generous or charitable out there, that charity or generosity extends in their places of work. Their generosity, like prosperity, thrives in an atmosphere of sincerity and integrity.

In closing, if you still doubt the magic formula of achieving prosperity through generosity, allow me to fill your heart with ancient words of wisdom that reverberate throughout the centuries:

"The wise man does not lay up his own treasures.
The more he gives to others, the more he has for himself."

Lao Tzu

REFERENCES

Anderson, Joel. "What $1,000 Invested in Stocks 10 Years Ago Would Be Worth Today." Yahoo Finance, October 7, 2020. https://finance.yahoo.com/news/1-000-stocks-invested-10-174000688.html.

Bankrate. "Financial Security Index." Accessed February 9, 2022. https://www.bankrate.com/financial-security-index/.

Benjamin, Michael O. The Power of Yet. Independently Published, 2019.

Bieber, Christy. "Pay Your Mortgage Early or Invest?" The Motley Fool, May 24, 2018. https://www.fool.com/mortgages/2018/05/24/pay-your-mortgage-early-or-invest.aspx.

Bundrick, Hal M., and Linda Bell. "Should I Pay Off My Mortgage?" NerdWallet, January 15, 2021. https://www.nerdwallet.com/article/mortgages/pay-off-mortgage.

Danna, Judy. "Houle Study: Which Students Have the Most College Loan Debt," December 12, 2013. https://sociology.dartmouth.edu/news/2013/12/houle-study-which-students-have-most-college-loan-debt.

Dixon, Amanda. "A Guide to Life Insurance Laddering." Smart Asset, February 13, 2019. https://smartasset.com/life-insurance/a-guide-to-life-insurance-laddering.

Fidelity Learning Center. "What Are Mutual Funds?" Accessed February 7, 2022. https://www.fidelity.com/learning-center/investment-products/mutual-funds/what-are-mutual-funds.

First Republic Bank. "U.S. Student Loan Debt Statistics," March 25, 2021. https://www.firstrepublic.com/personal-line-of-credit/student-loan-debt-averages-2021.

Frankel, Matthew. "Investing in REITs 101: The Pros and Cons." Million Acres, August 10, 2021. https://www.millionacres.com/real-estate-investing/reits/reit-investing-101/reit-investing-101-pros-cons/.

————. "What Is the Nasdaq Composite Index?" The Motley Fool, February 2, 2022. https://www.fool.com/investing/stock-market/indexes/nasdaq/.

Garcia, Adrian D. "Survey: Most Americans Wouldn't Cover a $1K Emergency with Savings." Bankrate, January 16, 2019. https://www.bankrate.com/banking/savings/financial-security-january-2019/

Ganti, Akhilesh, and Gordon Scott. "Dow Jones Industrial Average (DJIA)." Investopedia, January 3, 2022. https://www.investopedia.com/terms/d/djia.asp.

Hanson, Melanie. "Student Loan Debt Statistics." Education Data Initiative, January 27, 2022. https://educationdata.org/student-loan-debt-statistics.

Harvey, Catherine S. "Unlocking the Potential of Emergency Savings Accounts." AARP, October 2019. https://www.aarp.org/ppi/info-2019/unlocking-the-potential-of-emergency-savings-accounts.html.

Hasenstab, Maria. "Economic Literacy for Life." Federal Reserve Bank of St. Louis, May 5, 2017. https://www.stlouisfed.org/timely-topics/economic-literacy-for-life.

Hogan, Chris. Everyday Millionaires. Franklin, TN: Ramsey Press, 2019.

Hurley, Joseph F. The Best Way to Save for College : A Complete Guide to 529 Plans. 10th ed. Pittsford, NY: Bonacom, 2013.

Investopedia. "J.B. Maverick." Accessed February 7, 2022. https://www.investopedia.com/contributors/53889/.

Lalli, Frank. "How She Turned $5,000 into $22 Million (And How You Might Too...)." CNN Money, January 1, 1996. https://money.cnn.com/magazines/moneymag/moneymag_archive/1996/01/01/207651/index.htm.

Mastroeni, Tara. "REITs Are a Way to Own Real Estate without Becoming a Landlord—Here's How They Work, How to Invest, and the Different Kinds to Invest In." Business Insider Nederland, September 9, 2020. https://www.businessinsider.nl/reits-are-a-way-to-own-real-estate-without-becoming-a-landlord-heres-how-they-work-how-to-invest-and-the-different-kinds-to-invest-in/.

Minnesota Council on Economic Education. "Planning and Tracking Lesson 2A: The Inventory Game—Net Worth and Cash Flow Making Personal Finance," 2019. https://www.stlouisfed.org/~/media/education/curriculum/pdf/making-personal-finance-decisions-lesson-2a.pdf.

Morrissey, Monique. "The State of American Retirement Savings." Economic Policy Institute, December 10, 2019.

https://www.epi.org/publication/the-state-of-american-retirement-savings/.

National Institute of Retirement Security. "Financial Asset Inequality and Its Implications for Retirement Security," September 2019. https://www.nirsonline.org/reports/financial-asset-inequality-and-its-implications-for-retirement-security/.

Saving for College. "Mark Kantrowitz." Accessed February 9, 2022. https://www.savingforcollege.com/authors/mark-kantrowitz.

Segal, Troy. "Diversification." Investopedia, updated April 21, 2021. https://www.investopedia.com/terms/d/diversification.asp.

Settembre, Jeanette. "Retired Americans at Risk Financially as Wealth Gap Widens." Fox Business, October 31, 2019. https://www.foxbusiness.com/money/retired-americans-at-risk-finanically-as-wealth-gap-worsens.

Shorrocks, Anthony, James Davies, and Rodrigo Lluberas. "The Global Wealth Report 2020." Research Institute, 2020, 42. https://www.credit-suisse.com/media/assets/corporate/docs/about-us/research/publications/global-wealth-report-2020-en.pdf.

Smith, Keith Cameron. The Top 10 Distinctions Between Millionaires and the Middle Class. New York: Ballantine Books, 2007.

Spectrem Group. "Coronavirus Reduces Millionaire Count," March 23, 2020. https://spectrem.com/Content/millionaire-count-reduces.aspx.

Stratford, Michael. "Study: Student Debt Squeezes Middle Class the Most." Inside Higher Ed, December 11, 2013. https://www.insidehighered.com/quicktakes/2013/12/11/study-student-debt-squeezes-middle-class-most.

T. Rowe Price. "Munis May Be Attractive for Fixed Income Investors." Winter 2020 Issue: T. Rowe Price Investor® Magazine, 2020. https://www.troweprice.com/personal-investing/resources/insights/winter-2020-issue-t-rowe-price-investor-magazine.html.

Thompson, Chris. "Rule of 72 Defined." Smart Asset, September 1, 2020. https://smartasset.com/investing/what-is-the-rule-of-72.

U.S. Securities and Exchange Commission. "Municipal Bonds," April 28, 2021. https://www.investor.gov/introduction-investing/general-resources/news-alerts/alerts-bulletins/investor-bulletins/municipal.

———. "Mutual funds." Accessed February 10, 2022. https://www.investor.gov/introduction-investing/investing-basics/investment-products/mutual-funds-and-exchange-traded-1.

———. "Real Estate Investment Trusts (REITs)." Accessed February 9, 2022. https://www.investor.gov/introduction-investing/investing-basics/investment-products/real-estate-investment-trusts-reits.

ABOUT THE AUTHOR

Vergara Dean offers a multifaceted educational and professional experience highly suited for this book project. He started his Nursing career in the Bronx,NY as an ER Nurse at Lincoln Hospital & Medical Center. Dean earned his Nursing degree from Hostos Community College in the Bronx. He interned as a Legal Nurse Consultant at the Healthcare Bureau, NY State Attorney General's Office. Dean pursued his career in California - rose to become a Hospital Administrative Supervisor. In this capacity, Dean worked in various Hospitals where he learned of the healthcare workers' unmet needs for financial literacy.

Before migrating to the US, Dean was a Philippine government Legislative Liaison Specialist at the Dept. Of Foreign Affairs, and he was a Legal Officer at the country's former Energy Regulatory Board under the Office of the President.

Dean has a Juris Doctor degree from the University of Sto Tomas, Manila, and a BA degree from Naga City's seminary with the highest distinction as the recipient of the Rector's Award for Excellence in Philosophy.

Dean is an inaugural graduate of the University of California - Riverside Micro MBA Program while working at the Riverside County Hospital - University Health System Arlington campus.

Dean is married to a Kaiser Permanente Registered Nurse with 2 daughters.

He has a passion for cooking, gardening, and politics. He considers himself a lifetime student of personal finance and economics.